CONTENTS

I0570119

PART 1

AGAINST ALL ODDS

TRULY MOTIVATIONAL
FOOTBALL
STRIES
FOR KIDS

250 FUN SPORTS FACTS INCLUDED

20 OF THE MOST INSPIRATIONAL TRUE TALES FROM FOOTBALL'S GREATEST FOR YOUNG READERS & ACHIEVERS

ETHAN WILSON

NEW YORK JETS

BROADWAY JOE'S GUARANTEE IN SUPER BOWL III

The Super Bowl is the biggest game in football. All eyes in the sports world are watching the two teams who make it there. There are always plenty of storylines in the week leading up to the game. But leading up to Super Bowl III in January 1969, there was no bigger storyline than Joe Namath, the quarterback of the New York Jets, opening his mouth and guaranteeing a win over legendary head coach Don Shula, NFL MVP Earl Morrall, and the heavily favored Baltimore Colts.

Normally, Namath was "Joe Cool." He didn't really let anything get to him. If things weren't going his way, he just powered through and got the job done. And most of the time, he didn't react to anything that the media had to say. He just let it roll off his back. But at a media event at the Miami Touchdown Club three days before the big game, a loud, obnoxious Colts fan finally managed to get under Namath's skin. The fan heckled Joe, and told him that Baltimore, who was favored by almost three touchdowns, would smash the Jets. Without missing a beat, Namath faced the heckler and said, "We're going to win the game. I guarantee it."

In today's sports world, when an athlete guarantees that they'll win a game or contest, most people would probably see them as cocky. But if they can back it up, fans and history will see them differently. Joe Namath and the Jets would have to overcome a massive challenge if they wanted to make good on his guarantee and win a Super Bowl ring. Not only was Baltimore's expected margin of victory absolutely massive, the AFL was seen as an inferior league to the NFL. AFL players normally weren't as talented as those in the NFL.

The Colts rolled through the regular season on the way to an impressive 13-1 record, before shutting down the Minnesota Vikings and the Cleveland Browns in back-to-back playoff games. The Browns had been the only team to defeat the Colts in the regular season that year. But a 34-0 blowout victory over Cleveland sent the Colts to the Super Bowl. They looked invincible.

The Jets went 11-3 in the AFL, and managed to win the AFL Championship Game over the Oakland Raiders, 27-23. But the Jets weren't even the best team in the AFL in terms of record. How on earth did they expect to stand a chance against the Baltimore juggernaut? It was a true case of David vs. Goliath.

Jets head coach Weeb Ewbank was furious with Namath for guaranteeing a win over the Colts. Ewbank knew that his team was an underdog. He wanted the Jets to take a low-profile approach to the game. Ewbank confronted Namath the next morning. He couldn't believe it. Had Namath really guaranteed a win over the Colts in the Super Bowl? Without batting an eye, Namath told his head coach that he had. Ewbank ripped into his young quarterback: "Ah Joe, Joe Joe... You know what they're going to do? They're going to put that story up on the locker room wall. Those Colts are gonna want to kill us."

Namath's guarantee did motivate Baltimore to crush the AFL Champion Jets. But any motivation that the Colts gained paled in comparison to what that guarantee did for New York. All year long, the Jets had heard about how weak their league was. They had also seen what the Green Bay Packers had done to the AFL Champion team in Super Bowl I (a 35-10 blowout win over the Chiefs), and Super Bowl II (A 33-14 win over the Raiders).

By the time Namath made his now famous guarantee, the Jets weren't just focused and ready to go—they were angry. They were tired of hearing how they were going to get blown out by the supposedly invincible Baltimore Colts. And once the time came to play the game on January 12, 1969, they were locked and loaded. The New York Jets were rolling down the runway and cleared for takeoff!

The Jets weren't talented enough to go toe to toe with the Colts and beat them straight up. So they had to outsmart Don Shula and Baltimore to have a chance to win. One of the first things that they did was to use their top wide receiver Don Maynard as a decoy. Baltimore knew how dangerous Maynard was and double teamed him. But what the Colts didn't know was that Maynard was injured. He was playing hurt. They wasted coverage on him. This meant that another wide receiver, George Sauer Jr., was only being covered by one defender most of the day. He made Baltimore pay. He gashed their defense as he hauled in eight catches for 133 yards.

However, the Colts were still an extremely powerful team. They drove right down the field on their first possession of the game. They were poised to score a touchdown until the Jets defense stiffened up around their 20-yard line. But Baltimore missed a field goal, which kept the game scoreless early on. But this miss gave the Jets a massive confidence boost. They even held the Colts scoreless throughout the entire first quarter. The three-touchdown underdogs were holding their own against the NFL's best team!

In the second quarter, Joe Namath led the Jets on a methodical, steady 12-play, 80-yard touchdown drive to take a 7-0 lead! New York mixed up their play calls to keep the Colts defense confused and off balance. Along with making smart decisions with the football, the Jets also needed plenty of luck to have a chance in this one. Before halftime, the Colts had not one, but two prime chances to score. They probably should have blown the game wide open. After all, they were a much better team than the Jets were on paper. But the Super Bowl isn't won or lost on paper. It's won on the field, and Baltimore failed to capitalize on either of their scoring opportunities just before halftime. The Jets had life. They were up 7-0 on the most powerful football team in the world, and their confidence would only grow from there.

The Jets didn't blow the Colts out. Instead, they slowly drained the clock in the third quarter, played tough defense, and expanded their lead by kicking three field goals to make it 16-0 heading to the fourth quarter. By this point, Baltimore was in shock. They didn't know what to do. Weeb Ewbank had thoroughly outcoached Don Shula. Joe Namath played one of the best games of his life. And the Colts' NFL MVP, Earl Morrall, threw three interceptions that day. A stingy Jets defense never let him get going.

Don Shula became so frustrated that he benched Morrall later in the game in favor of the legendary quarterback Johnny Unitas. Unitas is one of the greatest quarterbacks in football history. But unfortunately for the Colts, Unitas was suffering from an elbow injury most of the year. He led Baltimore on one touchdown drive to make it a 16-7 game, but that was as close as the Colts would get the rest of the day. The Jets ran out the rest of the clock.

They had done it. The Jets made good on Joe Namath's guarantee. The victory over the Colts in the Super Bowl cemented Joe Namath's status as an all-time legend. The Jets also showed the rest of the sports world that teams from the American Football League could play with and beat teams from the NFL. The Jets earned respect not only for themselves, but for their league.

After the game, Joe Namath wouldn't talk to reporters in the locker room until he was finally forced to do so. He was very upset and angry that many of these same people doubted him and his team. But he still managed to take the moment in. He was now a World Champion quarterback.

When he finally answered questions from reporters, the man known as Broadway Joe, the larger-than-life celebrity, was quiet, humble and down to earth. He put his teammates ahead of himself when giving credit: "You've got to have confidence in your team. You've got to have confidence in yourself. And if you don't have that confidence, you can't play football. We all felt we could win. We won."

The reporter then asked Namath if he felt like he was king of the hill. And again, he shined the spotlight on his teammates instead of basking in it himself. "No, we're king of the hill. We've got the team, brother."

The 1969 New York Jets were heavy underdogs. But they never doubted their ability to succeed. And they were led by a man who had the heart, guts, and confidence to get them to where he knew they could go.

There's a fine line between confidence and cockiness. Stay humble in life. But when someone is pushing you around, making fun of you or your dreams, don't be afraid to push back. If you're going to succeed when you grow up, you need to believe in yourself. If you don't, who will? Believe in yourself. You'll fire people up just like Joe Namath fired up the Jets!

· The Jets' win in Super Bowl III over the Colts showed that the NFL and AFL were two equal football leagues. This eventually led to them combining, or merging in 1970 into the NFL we know today.

· Joe Namath signed a $427,000 contract in 1965 to play for the AFL's Jets instead of the NFL's Cardinals. This was the most lucrative deal for a rookie in history at the time.

· Some people thought his contract would ruin football. But it looks like it was worth it!

· Is one of just two players to win both a Super Bowl in professional football, and a national championship in college football. Joe Namath won with the New York Jets and Alabama, and Joe Montana won with the 49ers and Notre Dame.

· Joe Namath was the first quarterback in NFL history to pass for 4,000 yards when he did it in 1967.

· Earned his nickname "Broadway Joe" for his flashy, larger-than-life, outspoken personality.

· Inducted into the Pro Football Hall of Fame in 1985.

· Became a famous actor, and starred in movies and TV shows such as the Brady Bunch, the Simpsons, ALF, and the Dean Martin Show.

· Was well known for being unmarried in his late 30s, until he married his first wife Deborah Mays in 1984. They had two children, daughters Jessica and Olivia.

· He was born and raised in Beaver Falls, Pennsylvania, a blue-collar town. His father was a steelworker.

1. How many times was Joe Namath named an All-Star/Pro Bowler during his playing career?

2. What number did Joe Namath wear when he played for the Jets?

3. True or false: Joe Namath wrote a book talking about his life on and off the field?

4. What was the name of the Jets' coach who led the team to victory in Super Bowl III? It's a weird name.

5. True or false: Joe Namath briefly played baseball at the University of Alabama.

6. What was the name of the final team Joe Namath played for before retiring in 1977?

7. True or false: Joe Namath threw 200 career touchdown passes.

8. Who was the legendary college football coach that Joe Namath played for at Alabama?

9. True or false: Joe Namath played football even after retiring from the NFL.

10. True or false: Joe Namath once wore a fur coat to a game.

ANSWER

1. *Five times.*
2. *#12*
3. *True. His book is simply called Namath: A Biography.*
4. *Weeb Ewbank.*
5. *True. Joe was quite the athlete at Alabama before he settled on football.*
6. *The Los Angeles Rams.*
7. *false. He threw 173 career touchdown passes.*
8. *Paul "Bear" Bryant.*
9. *True. He played for a league called the World Football league in 1983.*
10. *True. He once wore a fur coat to a game against the Baltimore Colts, when it was freezing cold at just 16 degrees!*

"When you have confidence, you can have a lot of fun. And when you have fun, you can do amazing things."

"If you aren't going all the way, why go at all?"

"A champion needs a motivation above and beyond winning."

"To be a leader, you have to make people want to follow you, and nobody wants to follow someone who doesn't know where he is going."

"I believe in discipline; I believe in respect; I believe in those characteristics that help you attain greatness in life."

LESSONS FROM STORY

• The Jets were a heavy underdog to Baltimore, and sports reporters laughed at Joe Namath's guarantee. But his guarantee of victory actually fired up his teammates. Belief in yourself can fire you and other people up!

• Nobody gave the Jets a chance to win. But they won anyway. Even if no one else believes in you, believe in yourself anyway.

• Even if you're not as talented as somebody, you can outsmart them and outwork them. The Jets were not as talented as the Colts. But they outsmarted Baltimore in several different ways. Talent rarely beats intelligence and hard work.

• Joe Namath kept his cool under pressure. When you're going through a tough situation, keep your cool as best as you can. Panicking doesn't solve anything.

• Be confident in yourself, but humble in both victory and defeat.

DAMON SHEEHY-GUISEPPI

NOT TAKING NO FOR AN ANSWER

We all have dreams growing up. Perhaps we have a dream to be an actor, an astronaut, or a world-famous athlete in any sport. But for Damon Sheehy-Guiseppi, all he wanted was a chance. A chance to show what he could do. He had some athletic ability, but he knew that he wasn't a superstar. But the lengths that he would go to, to make an NFL team, would inspire people everywhere!

His NFL dream began when he failed to live out another dream. Damon started out wanting to be an NBA player. Basketball was his sport growing up. But at only 5'11 and 175 pounds, he wasn't built for the sport. He didn't have the size. Damon enjoyed playing the game in high school in Lake Havasu, Arizona. But he wasn't even ranked as a college basketball prospect. He wasn't on the radar of college basketball scouts. So he decided to try out for the basketball team at Mesa Community College in Mesa, Arizona. There was just one problem: he didn't make the team.

However, instead of doing what a lot of people do, and letting that brick wall stop him in his tracks, Damon took his first detour. If he couldn't go through the wall, he would go around it. He tried out for the school's track team instead. He might not have had the body or talent to be a star basketball player. But Damon did have speed. Lots of it. He was blazing fast! When he was on the Mesa Community College track team, he looked like he was well on his way to succeeding there until another obstacle smacked him in the face. Damon was unfortunately involved in a car accident.

This prematurely ended his track season. Most people would have probably given up. Failing to make a community college basketball team, having a track career sidelined with a freak accident, and living a hard life would be too much to handle for most people. But Damon Sheehy-Guiseppi wasn't like most people. He was stubborn. He knew his dream was worth chasing. He wanted to make it to the NFL. So, he simply kept his spirits up, stayed positive, continued to train, and kept himself ready for the next opportunity. And his next chance would come sooner than he thought.

Damon soon found out about a football tryout for Phoenix College. He went to the tryout and gave it everything he had. He ran his fastest, went through each drill to the best of his ability, and left it all out on the field. Except the team never called Damon back to let him know whether he'd made the roster. That didn't bother him. He may not have heard a "yes" from the scouts at the tryout. But he also never heard the word "no" either. So he did what anyone truly chasing their dream would do: he showed up to the next practice with the team.

Damon figured that if he didn't make the roster, he would be told to leave by the coaching staff. If that happened, he would simply leave, and keep searching for his next opportunity. But if they let him practice, that would give him another chance to show what he could do on the gridiron. As luck would have it, the coaches let Damon practice. And he showed up to every single summer practice for Phoenix College and gave it everything he had. He was one of the fastest players on the team too! Whether it was sprinting, receiving drills, special teams drills, or anything else, Damon did all that was asked of him. He went above and beyond. And before he knew it, he earned a roster spot!

Once he was playing for the Phoenix College Bears, Damon took off. He was a special teams sensation at the junior college level. He was a truly dangerous return man, racking up over 1,200 yards returning kickoffs and punts. He did so well that he became an All-American. The next season, he was even better, gaining 1,278 yards and running back four kickoffs for touchdowns. He even added 400 punt return yards on top of that. He was the best return man in the country!

Damon didn't look like a natural football player before he got his chance. He was so used to playing basketball, and didn't initially have the experience returning kickoffs and punts. But now that he had his chance, he was making the most of it. He was tough as nails, blazing fast, and had the heart of a lion! But just when Damon thought his dream was about to take off, his football days with Phoenix College were over. His journey had hit a peak. And he was unfortunately about to go down into one of the deepest valleys of his life.

Even though he tore it up in the junior college level playing football, no bigger schools would sign him. After that, he had tryouts with the Miami Dolphins and the Tampa Bay Buccaneers. He didn't make it on their rosters either. He even tried the Canadian Football League and Arena Football League. He had absolutely horrible luck.

What's worse is that Damon had started to max out a credit card trying to be able to afford going to all these tryouts and camps. He was running out of money. Fast. He was even down to playing flag football. No pro teams wanted him and he was getting poorer by the day. He hit rock bottom. Until one of his teammates directed him to the place where he would finally get his shot in the NFL.

Damon's flag football teammate relayed to him that the Cleveland Browns were holding a tryout in Miami. Off he went. He got the address for the camp, drove to Miami, and looked for Alonzo Highsmith, one of the Browns' executives. When he met with Alonzo, Damon charmed his way into the camp even though he hadn't been invited. He was just crazy and gutsy enough to act like he knew Alonzo. It worked. He made it into the camp. But he still wasn't part of the team's roster yet.

He had also run out of money by this point. He was sleeping in gyms, outside in sleeping bags, and struggling to find his next meal at times. It was now or never. Either Damon would make the Browns roster and find a steady place to live, a steady paycheck for the next few months, and food to eat. Or he would have to find a way back home to Arizona with literally nothing in his pockets. However, Damon wowed Alonzo Highsmith with his speed, courage and tireless work ethic. This even caught the attention of Browns General Manager John Dorsey, who was responsible for signing and drafting new players to Cleveland's roster.

Damon had made it to Cleveland for the team's official camp. But he was tired, hungry, and had no money in his pockets. Somehow, some way, whether it was by sheer willpower or by an act of God, he ran a 4.38 40-yard dash with John Dorsey, Alonzo Highsmith, and all the coaches watching him. Damon ran the fastest he'd ever ran in his life. This unknown special teamer from Lake Havasu, Arizona, ended up being faster than most of the best wide receivers in the upcoming NFL Draft. That was enough. That earned him a free agent contract. Damon had done it. He was officially a Cleveland Brown!

This story ends on a slightly sad note though. While Damon did earn a free agent contract, he unfortunately didn't make it to the official 53-man roster for the start of the 2019 season. He was cut in the preseason. It is incredibly difficult for a player to make it onto a team's official roster. And this is true even for the ones who get drafted. So, the fact that Damon was in this position at all was a miracle.

Damon was with the Browns only for a short time. But he won over the entire team with his work ethic, positive attitude, and desire to do his very best. He even scored an 86-yard touchdown on a punt return against the Washington Redskins in a preseason game! The entire Browns team went nuts after he scored! The team's bench cleared, and everybody celebrated with him in the endzone!

Damon Sheehy-Guiseppi is living proof that hard work can accomplish anything. He wanted to be an NFL player. And because of his relentless work ethic, he became one. It does not matter how impossible your dreams may seem. It does not matter what the naysayers tell you. If you have a lifelong dream that you are aching to accomplish, go for it. Do whatever it takes.

Damon Sheehy-Guiseppi gave just about everything to accomplish his dream. He was briefly homeless, hungry, and exhausted. But he wanted to accomplish his dream badly enough. And he didn't stop until he'd achieved it. Don't stop until you've achieved yours!

· Played in the XFL with the New York Guardians in 2019, and in the CFL with the Ottawa Redblacks in 2021.

· Currently plays for the Legnano Frogs of the Italian Football League.

· Superstar wide receiver Odell Beckham Jr. let him borrow his shoes for the preseason game against the Redskins...and those were the same shoes he wore when he scored the touchdown!

· Was briefly homeless until he made it onto the Browns.

· Before his impressive tryout with Cleveland in 2019, he hadn't played football since 2016.

· Scored as many as six punt return touchdowns in one season in college.

· He wanted a shot at playing in the NFL so badly, that he told Browns executive Alonzo Highsmith that he had played at a historically black college in Virginia, and that he had trained with former NFL players. It wasn't true. But it worked to get his foot in the door.

· He was once struggling so much, that his family and friends had to send him food they ordered online.

· His ability to instantly change direction when he played basketball, helped him become an explosively quick football player.

· Set to play as a punt returner for the Legnano Frogs of the Italian Football League for the 2024 season.

1. True or false: Damon-Sheehy Guiseppi ran the 40-yard dash in 4.4 seconds.

2. True or false: Damon Sheehy Guiseppi also played in the CFL and XFL.

3. True or false: Damon Sheehy-Guiseppi's original dream was to be an NBA superstar.

4. True or false: The Browns invited him to minicamp with them.

5. True or false: He briefly played football for Arizona State.

6. True or false: In addition to playing football and basketball, he also tried to do track and field.

7. True or false: Damon's story is famous in the football world.

8. True or false: Damon was born in Arizona.

9. True or false: Damon has a younger brother who is a college basketball player.

10. True or false: Damon attended high school in Arizona.

ANSWER

1. *False, he ran it in 4.38 seconds, which is extremely fast!*
2. *True. He played for the Ottawa Redblacks and the New York Guardians.*
3. *True. He's an explosive return man, but he really wanted to play in the NBA before finding football.*
4. *False. He got the information from a teammate, and made his way to Miami for the tryout.*
5. *False. He never played Division I college football.*
6. *True! Track and field helped Damon discover his speed.*
7. *True! He was interviewed by CBS Sports, NFL Network and Rich Eisen, a famous football analyst.*
8. *False. He was born in Orlando, Florida.*
9. *True! Damon's younger brother Dylan Guiseppi plays as a guard on the VCU (Virginia Commonwealth University) men's basketball team.*
10. *Answer: False, he moved all the way from Arizona to Michigan to attend St. Francis High School.*

"It's just a blessing. I've come a long way, and before I was just trying to get in the door, and now the door is calling me in."

"Two years ago, I was trying to get in the AAF, and I couldn't get in there. Now to get a call like, 'Do you want to be in the XFL?' is just such a blessing."

"My focus is to win in everything I can possibly do."

"I slept on the grass right outside the facility to make sure I didn't miss a tryout."

"Keep going. Just keep working hard if it's your dream. There's nothing in the world you can't do. You make your own destiny. You can do whatever you want in this life."

LESSONS FROM STORY

· If at first you don't succeed, try, try, and try again.

· Life doesn't usually go according to plan. Winners find a way to make things happen during the detours!

· If you want a dream bad enough, give everything you have. You may or may not succeed. But at least you'll have no regrets.

· Chase your passion like Damon chased his. Making it onto a professional football team was his dream. Even though he's now in the Italian Football League instead of the NFL, he's still living his dream.

· Don't let the naysayers tell you can't do something because you're not fast enough, talented enough or smart enough. Hard work trumps everything else.

EMMITT SMITH
DRIVEN TO SUCCEED

The most successful people in life are the ones who use everything as fuel to push themselves. This fuel could be people telling them they can't do something. It could be overcoming inner struggles to be a better person, or it could simply be a desire to be better than they were yesterday.

Hall of Fame running back Emmitt Smith thrived on driving himself to succeed any way he could. That's why he's now a football legend. But it wasn't always this way. Emmitt tore up the field as a running back for the Escambia High School Gators. He rushed for an unheard of 8,804 yards and 106 touchdowns, while leading Escambia to a pair of State Championships. But in spite of his incredible ability as a running back, Smith was doubted and even criticized.

The main complaints that scouts had about him were that he was supposedly too small and slow to play running back in college. The harshest criticism came from recruiting expert Max Emfinger, who tore Smith down when he signed on to play college football at the University of Florida: "Emmitt Smith is a lugger, not a runner. He's not fast. He can't get around the corner. When he falls flat on his face, remember where you heard it first."

Along with fuel like that driving him toward success, Smith also learned something from his high school head coach that he would take with him throughout the rest of his life, both on and off the football field. Escambia head coach Dwight Thomas once instructed his players to write their top three goals for the football team on an index card, and then put the card in their locker so they would be able to see their goals each day. "It's a dream until you write it down, and then it becomes a goal," Coach Thomas said.

Emmitt took Coach Thomas's advice to heart. He used that while he was at the University of Florida, and before long, he was lighting it up in Gainesville. He didn't start for the Gators until the third game of his college career. But once he got his first chance to carry the football, he never looked back.

In his first career start in 1987 against Alabama, Emmitt didn't just have a good day, he smashed an old rushing record that had stood since 1930! He was only a freshman running back, and he broke Red Bethea's rushing record at Florida for rushing yards in a single game with 224 yards and two touchdowns! Emmitt Smith had sent a loud and clear message to the rest of the college football world. It was almost as if his running style told opposing defenses, "I'm here. And I dare you to try and stop me!"

Even though Emmitt was only 5'9 and 216 pounds, he ran with the power and authority of a 240-pound bruiser. He was extremely tough to tackle. He often ran straight through opposing players who tried to tackle him. Teams were rarely able to bring him down with just one defender. They often had to gang up on Emmitt to have any chance to succeed against him. He was proving all the naysayers dead wrong. Even as a freshman at Florida, Emmitt put the rest of America on notice. He ran for 1,348 yards that season, and reached 1,000 yards in just his seventh career game, which is the fastest any running back in college football history has reached that mark!

He suffered a sprained knee the next season, which slowed him down a bit. But his junior year in 1989 was a breakout year. Emmitt set several Florida records that season, including the longest run (96 yards vs. Mississippi State), rushing yards in a season (1,599 yards), career rushing touchdowns (36), and many others.

However, Emmitt left Florida before the 1990 season because he felt like he wouldn't be used much that year. The Gators just hired a new football coach named Steve Spurrier, who was more interested in throwing the football instead of running it. So Emmitt declared for the 1990 NFL Draft. But what if I told you he wasn't Dallas's first choice?

The Cowboys were coming off an awful 1-15 season in 1989, and were focused on rebuilding their defense first. But when the Bengals took the player they wanted, and Emmitt was still there by the time they had a chance to pick him at #17, it was a no-brainer. The Cowboys grabbed their soon-to-be franchise running back, and were ready to make their climb to Super Bowl glory! Emmitt made an impact right away. As a rookie in 1990, he ran for 937 yards and 11 touchdowns, and he was named the Rookie of the Year, and made his first Pro Bowl.

Interestingly enough, making the Pro Bowl was one of Emmitt's goals for the 1990 season. One day when Emmitt was playing dominoes with his teammate James Washington in the locker room, Washington discovered Emmitt's goal sheet when he attempted to use it for a piece of paper to keep score. On the paper it said: 1990 Season Goals: Make the Pro Bowl, be the NFL's leading rusher, and be the team MVP.

It was then that Washington and other Cowboys learned how serious Emmitt was about his future. He didn't just want to have a solid career in the NFL—he wanted to be the greatest running back of all time. And when Emmitt got serious about success, so did the Cowboys. They rebounded from a pair of bad seasons in 1989 and 1990 to make the playoffs in 1991 and win their first postseason game in over a decade. But 1992 and 1993 would be truly special for Emmitt and the Cowboys as they would win back-to-back Super Bowls. Emmitt would even be named both NFL MVP and Super Bowl MVP, too!

Two years later, Emmitt would win yet another Super Bowl. At this point in his career, he had nothing left to prove. He was a three-time Super Bowl Champion, and was an eventual Hall of Famer. But he had one goal left to accomplish. He set this goal for himself when he first came into the NFL in 1990: Be the league's all-time leading rusher.

He passed elite company as he worked his way up the ladder. Thurman Thomas. Franco Harris. Jim Brown. Barry Sanders. Emmitt passed them all. And he finally claimed the all-time rushing record in 2002, with 17,162 yards. After playing the final two years of his career with the Arizona Cardinals, Emmitt's final career rushing yards total was an astonishing 18,355 yards. He also has the NFL record for the most rushing touchdowns ever, with 164. And this was all accomplished by a man who scouts said was too slow, too small, and not fit to play big-time college football, let alone NFL football. So many people doubted Emmitt Smith. But he made them all look like fools as he became one of the greatest running backs of all time. And this was all because of his work ethic, and accomplishing the goals that he set for himself.

Emmitt truly showed why he was the one of the greats when he was inducted into the Pro Football Hall of Fame in

2010. Instead of showing off or gloating about making it in, he spent the majority of his speech thanking others, from his quarterback Troy Aikman, to wide receiver Michael Irvin, to the fullback who blocked for him, Darryl Johnston. Emmitt spent more time thanking them than talking about his own accomplishments.

He also left a wise piece of advice for anyone who wants to succeed in life, no matter what they do. Emmitt said: "Claim your inner champion. When you claim your inner champion, you learn to see, hear and feel differently than others. So what I most want to convey here is: Never let others define you. You define yourself."

Has anyone told you that you're not good enough, strong enough, or smart enough to accomplish something? If they have, use that as fuel to push toward your dream. The naysayers don't know how hard you've had to work. They only see what everybody else sees. Let your hard work define you, and let your ultimate goal guide you on your journey to success. That's the Emmitt Smith way.

· Emmitt runs his own charity with his wife Pat, called Pat & Emmitt Smith Charities, which provides life experiences and educational opportunities to underprivileged youth.

· He won the third season of *Dancing with the Stars* in 2006.

· Emmitt started up a real estate company with one of his Cowboys teammates to help transform land in heavily populated areas.

· His wife is a former Miss Virginia winner. They have five children together.

· Since retiring from football, Emmitt has worked as an analyst and commentator for ESPN and NFL Network.

· He's the only running back in NFL history to rush for at least 1,000 yards in 11 consecutive seasons.

· Emmitt's brother Emory Smith also played in the NFL as a fullback.

· While he's known as a running back, Emmitt Smith was also a solid pass catcher out of the backfield, recording over 500 catches during his time in the NFL.

· He had his number, 22, retired by the Dallas Cowboys. It's only one of four numbers retired by the team.

· Emmitt's not just a football player. He's an author too! He's written two books, *The Emmitt Zone*, and *Game On: Find Your Purpose-Pursue Your Dream*.

1. True or false: Emmitt Smith won the Heisman Trophy in college for the University of Florida in 1989.

2. True or false: Emmitt Smith won three MVP titles.

3. How many times was Emmitt Smith named to the Pro Bowl during his career?

4. How many years did Emmitt Smith play in the NFL?

5. True or false: Emmitt Smith has over 20,000 career rushing yards.

6. How many Super Bowl rings does Emmitt Smith have?

7. Who did Emmitt Smith pass to become the NFL's all-time leading rusher?

8. True or false: Emmitt Smith has a biography written about him.

9. What year was Emmitt Smith inducted into the Pro Football Hall of Fame?

10. True or false: Emmitt Smith scored 150 rushing touchdowns in his career.

ANSWER

1. False. For as talented as he was, Emmitt Smith never won the Heisman Trophy. Andre Ware won the Heisman in 1989 for Houston.
2. False. Emmitt Smith has one MVP title in 1993.
3. He was named to the Pro Bowl eight times.
4. Emmitt Smith played in the NFL for 15 years with the Dallas Cowboys and Arizona Cardinals.
5. False. Emmitt Smith has 18,355 career rushing yards.
6. Emmitt Smith has three Super Bowl rings.
7. Walter Payton.
8. True. His biography was written by Ted Cox, and is called Emmitt Smith: Finding Daylight.
9. He was inducted into the Hall of Fame in 2010, his first year of eligibility.
10. False. Emmitt scored 164 rushing touchdowns in his career.

QUOTES

"Your goals are priceless, so don't undervalue them. Make them big enough to inspire you, and you'll rise to the occasion."

"Don't limit yourself. Many people limit themselves to what they think they can do. You can go as far as your mind lets you. What you believe, remember, you can achieve."

"Champions aren't made in gyms. Champions are made from something they have deep inside them—a desire, a dream, a vision."

"Greatness is not a destination; it's a journey that requires consistency, commitment, and hard work."

"Believe in yourself and all that you are. Know that there is something inside you that is greater than any obstacle."

LESSONS FROM STORY

· Consistency is key. Set goals, stick to them, and achieve them.

· Succeeding is not about how strong or talented you are. It's about refusing to give up, no matter what obstacle is in your way.

· Your dreams are just dreams until you write them down. Then they become goals.

· Don't listen to the naysayers.

· Work ethic can make up for a lot of weaknesses.

PART 2

SHOOT FOR THE STARS

THE DALLAS COWBOYS AND THE WORLD'S MOST FAMOUS HAIL MARY

The Hail Mary is a commonly known football play today. When a team has no other options left, and their backs are really against the wall, they might call this play in the huddle. It's simple: A team's wide receivers all just try to outrun the defensive backs to the end zone on a straight route. Then if he has time, the quarterback just throws up a prayer out of desperation, hoping that one of his receivers comes down with the ball. The chances that the ball is caught are slim to none. But if the play works? It can live in sports history forever!

The Hail Mary pass has existed for almost as long as the game of football has been around. But in the case of the NFL, the most famous Hail Mary in the league's history occurred on December 28, 1975. In that playoff game, the fourth-seeded Dallas Cowboys were a heavy underdog against the Minnesota Vikings.

The Vikings went 12-2 that year in the regular season, and started off the year with a 10-game winning streak. That was enough to get people in Minnesota dreaming of the Super Bowl. Dallas on the other hand, didn't even win the NFC East that year. They had a 10-4 record going into the playoffs, but lost out on winning the division by one game. As a result, Roger Staubach and his teammates were forced to head to freezing cold Minnesota to put their season on the line.

The 1975 NFC Divisional Playoff Game between the Vikings and Cowboys was a classic defensive battle. Dallas's famous Doomsday Defense held Fran Tarkenton and Minnesota in check for the whole first half. But the Vikings still managed to score a touchdown to go into the locker room with a 7-0 halftime lead. From there, Dallas came right out of the locker room and scored their first touchdown of the day when running back Doug Dennison powered the ball into the end zone after a long, steady drive. The Cowboys were back in it with the NFC's best team, and even briefly took a 10-7 lead with a field goal.

But after Minnesota came back to retake the lead with an 11-play, 70-yard touchdown drive, Dallas found themselves trailing yet again. They were down 14-10 with 5:24 remaining in the game. To make matters worse for the Cowboys, they went three and out on their next drive, and Minnesota forced Dallas to use all three timeouts after getting a stop on defense. By the time Dallas got the ball back, there was only 1:51 left remaining in the game.

The Vikings were now daring the Cowboys to march 91 yards against their unbeatable defense. Roger Staubach was one of the most famous athletes in the world at that time. But even he had never been in this position before. But his legend would soon grow, after leading the Cowboys on one of the most clutch drives in NFL history.

To start off the drive, Staubach hit Drew Pearson for two completions to move the ball to Dallas's 31-yard line. But then disaster nearly struck when he fumbled the snap and was tackled for a six-yard loss. Minnesota's defense stiffened up, and before long, the Cowboys were facing a 4th and 16. They had to convert or their season would be over. It was the end of the line—do or die.

But like all NFL legends do, Roger Staubach came up with the clutch play. He avoided the pass rush and uncorked another clutch pass to Drew Pearson. This one went for 25 yards, and set the Cowboys up to really go after Minnesota's defense. They no longer had their backs against the wall. They were in attack mode. And they had the chance to deliver the dagger.

After Preston Pearson dropped a wide-open pass, the next play would make NFL history. With 32 seconds left in the game, and Dallas's season hanging in the balance, Roger Staubach took the snap, set his feet, and fired a 50-yard dart to Drew Pearson down the right sideline. Pearson shielded the ball from Vikings cornerback Nate Wright, caught the pass, and backpedaled into the endzone. Touchdown, Cowboys!

There are bitter and angry Vikings fans almost 50 years later who will still say Drew Pearson pushed off on Nate Wright when he caught the game-winning touchdown. But their anger falls on deaf ears. Roger Staubach's pass to Drew Pearson will forever be known as one of the most clutch plays in NFL history. But it's what happened next that gave the pass its famous name.

In the locker room following the game, the reporter asked Roger Staubach what he was thinking when he let the ball fly. He had a simple answer, but it would change football forever: "I just closed my eyes and said a Hail Mary. I'm a Catholic kid from Cincinnati."

In the Catholic faith, a Hail Mary is a prayer asking for Mary, the mother of Jesus, to intervene on behalf of the person who is praying. But after Staubach told the reporter what was going through his mind on that play, the name stuck. Even though the play happened several times in the past before that, Staubach's game-winning touchdown was what made the name popular.

Staubach and the 1975 Cowboys played during a time when the game was focused on strong rushing attacks, and bruising tough defenses. The NFL back then is not the same sport we see today. Teams rarely threw passes that long, and certainly didn't have them in the playbook in the mid-1970s.

Roger Staubach probably wasn't thinking about how one desperation play would change football forever. He was just trying to help his team win, and advance to the next round of the playoffs. But today, in the NFL's pass-first game, every team has at least one (if not several) variations on the Hail Mary play. The Hail Mary has also made it into the common English language. When people mention a "Hail Mary" in life, they mean something that has a very slim chance of happening, with a huge reward if it does.

Like going out with the cutest girl or guy in school, or getting a big new job when everyone else is competing for it, a Hail Mary working out in these situations would also be almost as exciting as the football version of a Hail Mary! But beyond all the interesting language surrounding the Hail Mary pass, two huge lessons can be learned here: Trusting your teammates and believing in your ability to make great things happen.

The Hail Mary may be a desperation play, but a quarterback has to have trust in his teammates to catch his throw, even if there's little to no chance of succeeding. Not only that, but the quarterback also has to believe in himself to be able to make that throw. If neither of those things are there, there is no way that the Hail Mary play will work.

Do you believe in yourself? Do you have the talent to make your dream become a reality? Do you trust the people around you like your friends and family, to support you? If you do, you'll be able to succeed even when things are the hardest. You'll be able to make things happen even in a tight spot. You'll be like Roger Staubach was on that fateful day late in 1975. You'll be fearless, focused, ready to get the job done, and ready to go to work. The Hail Mary: One of the greatest plays not just in American football but in all of sports.

· The name of the Hail Mary play comes from the Catholic prayer that is also called a Hail Mary, asking for help from Mary, the mother of Jesus.

· They have an extremely low success rate. They don't usually work. But when they do, they often create spectacular football moments, just like the one in the story.

· Hail Mary passes typically have a success rate of less than 10%.

· During a Hail Mary play, the offense usually sends five wide receivers down the field, while the defense plays the Prevent formation, to stop a big play.

· While the 1975 Hail Mary thrown by Roger Staubach is the most famous example of the play, the pass evolved from any desperation play, or long pass.

· Hail Mary competitions are sometimes held as part of a skills challenge to see who can throw the longest pass.

· Roger Staubach coined the term because he is a devout Catholic.

· The name "Hail Mary" for a football play may have actually come from the 1922 Notre Dame football team. In a game against Georgia Tech, the players supposedly said the Hail Mary prayer before scoring plays. They won the game 13-3.

· Drew Pearson was the one who caught Roger Staubach's Hail Mary pass.

· The term Hail Mary can be used to describe anything that has a low chance of succeeding.

1. Along with the 1975 Cowboys, there was one other team who was known for using the Hail Mary to win games. They were nicknamed the Kardiac Kids. Which team is it?

2. Who threw the game-winning Hail Mary pass against the Miami Hurricanes in 1984?

3. Who first used the term "Hail Mary" in broadcasting to describe last-second desperation passes?

4. When did the NFL first officially recognize the Hail Mary as a play in its rules?

5. What is the minimum number of yards a pass needs to travel before it's considered a Hail Mary by most football experts?

6. Which famous coach once said when describing a Hail Mary play, "The only thing the Prevent defense prevents, is winning"?

7. Which quarterback threw the longest completed Hail Mary pass of 61 yards in 2015?

8. Which team attempted the first recorded Hail Mary pass in NFL history?

9. Who is the only quarterback to throw two successful game-winning Hail Mary passes in his career?

10. Which team executed a lateral-filled play that started with a Hail Mary, to beat the New England Patriots in 2018?

ANSWER

1. The 1980 Cleveland Browns
2. Doug Flutie. It became so famous that it was nicknamed the "Hail Flutie" pass.
3. Tom Hedrick, a producer for NFL Films, coined the phrase.
4. 1989.
5. 40 yards.
6. John Madden.
7. Aaron Rodgers.
8. The San Francisco 49ers did in 1957, even though the term Hail Mary had not been used at the time.
9. Couch led the Cleveland Browns to victory with not one, but two successful Hail Mary passes in 1999 over the New Orleans Saints, and 2002 over the Jacksonville Jaguars.
10. Miami Dolphins.

FIVE QUOTES ABOUT THE HAIL MARY PASS

"You used to have a wing and a prayer. Now the Hail Mary is used for politics, for business and for football." -Roger Staubach

"Without the Hail Mary pass, I think I could've very easily been forgotten. That pass put this label on me as the 'never over until it's over guy'. -Doug Flutie.

"It's the ultimate playground play. You just throw it up and see what happens." -Tony Romo

"It's the most exhilarating play in football. You just hope your guy comes down with it." -Troy Aikman.

"It's kind of a desperation play. It's not something you practice a whole lot." -Matthew Stafford

LESSONS FROM STORY

· Nothing is over until the final seconds, either in football or in life. Take your shot and chase your dream while you can!

· Trust in yourself and in others around you in both life and in sports.

· Believe in your ability to succeed, even against long odds.

· Practice, confidence and opportunity are three things in life that you need to have if you want to make difficult things happen.

· Positive visualization is one of the strongest forces there is!

BRANDON BURLSWORTH
THE WALK-ON

Some of the greatest superstars in NFL history were born with a ridiculous amount of God-given athletic ability. Night after night, they create highlight after highlight. They're shown on ESPN over and over again. But some of football's best and most inspiring players are forced to dig deep. Many did not win the "athletic lottery" and they are forced to play the hand that they're dealt by life. Brandon Burlsworth was one of those players.

Growing up in Harrison, Arkansas, Burlsworth had the passion to play football ever since he was a boy. But he lacked the talent for the game. According to his brother Marty Burlsworth, "There wasn't a whole lot of athletic ability. Not a great athlete." His high school coach Tommy Tice was blunt too. "He was slow. He was soft. We didn't think he'd ever play."

He didn't start on the football team until his junior year at Harrison High School. And even after he was an All-State player his senior year, none of the big schools were interested in him. He had only two or three offers to play college football at NCAA Division II schools.

Most football players would have taken a Division II scholarship offer. It would mean a free education, and a chance to set themselves up for later in life. But Brandon Burlsworth didn't take that path. He took the road less traveled, and decided to walk on at the University of Arkansas. He had grown up a Razorbacks football fan, and wanted to make his unlikely dream a reality.

But when Burlsworth first made that decision to join the Razorback football team as a walk-on, he was a long way away from where he wanted to be. He might have had the size and frame to be an offensive lineman. But he was a big guy when he first got to Arkansas in 1994. And it wasn't the good kind of big. He weighed 300 pounds, but he wasn't muscular. He was fat and extremely out of shape.

The naysayers and doubters were everywhere. Everyone from his coaches to his teammates doubted him. They all said something similar to this: "This kid will never play a down of football at the University of Arkansas." But Brandon had already chosen his path. There was no quitting or turning back. He had decided to go to one of the biggest schools in the country. And he wasn't about to let something like doubt stop him. But his journey to achieving his dream wasn't going to be easy. It would be brutal, backbreaking work. But the spark inside him wasn't going to be extinguished by anyone.

Once he was on the Arkansas campus, Brandon woke up at 5:15 every morning to lift weights. He was always the first one in the weight room, and the last one out. It also didn't matter what kind of day the Razorbacks were having in practice, he was always disciplined. He was even so focused on the task at hand that he never even took his helmet off. Not even during breaks. And long after his teammates had left for the day, Brandon would still be out on the practice field, going through his footwork, hand placement, and figuring out how to best explode out of his stance.

Being an offensive lineman is a very detail-oriented job on a football team. The best linemen do the little things right. If they don't, that's not only a big problem for them, it could mean that opposing defenses sack their quarterback on gameday. Brandon would never let that happen if he ever got the chance to play. So he continued to work, work, and work some more.

Brandon stayed after practice so often that one night, Arkansas head coach Houston Nutt caught him practicing his footwork in the dark at the Razorbacks' indoor practice facility. The lights were all off. It was pitch black in there. But that didn't matter to Brandon. He was focused on being the best offensive lineman and teammate he could possibly be. That was all that mattered to him.

"Didn't have a real good day today, Coach," he said. "I just want to make sure I got everything, just stepping through these plays."

And from that point on, Brandon's work ethic not only inspired Coach Nutt, but it also inspired the rest of the coaching staff and his teammates. His college roommate, wide receiver Anthony Lucas, recalls that Brandon truly helped build a sense of togetherness in the Arkansas football team not just on the field, but more importantly off it: "That year, a lot of things changed. Brandon just touched those guys," Anthony said. "We started going to bible study, we started doing a lot of things together. And it was just amazing the effect he had on us."

Coach Nutt even instilled a saying in his teams that honored Burlsworth long after his playing days at Arkansas: Do it the Burls way. This meant showing up to practice early, leaving late, studying game film as much as possible, working to exhaustion in the weight room, and playing for the guy next to them.

Before long, the camaraderie that Brandon Burlsworth had helped build on the team began to translate to wins. After bad seasons in 1996 and 1997, the 1998 Arkansas Razorbacks posted a surprising 9-3 record, including a blowout win over #22 Alabama that really put the rest of America on notice! Not only that, but the Razorbacks' success also attracted the attention of NFL scouts, who were considering drafting Burlsworth. The humble, quiet kid from Harrison, Arkansas was on the doorstep of making his dream bigger than he had ever imagined. All he wanted was to play football for Arkansas, the team he loved as a kid.

But that was under his belt now. He was a senior offensive lineman, an All-American, and was now squarely in the sights of NFL teams who were looking to build around him as a cornerstone for the future. And as fate would have it, the Indianapolis Colts selected Burlsworth with the 63rd overall pick of the 1999 NFL Draft.

The Colts were still struggling to rebuild. But they had taken young gunslinger Peyton Manning first overall in 1998, and were focused on rebuilding their offensive line this time around. Brandon Burlsworth was Indy's lineman of the future. Except he never got the chance to fill that role.

Along with being a top-notch football player, Brandon Burlsworth was also a devout Christian. His faith inspired everything he did, from how he treated others, to how hard he worked. And whenever he was home, he would always go to church with his mother, Barbara Burlsworth. Eleven days after being drafted, he was headed home to Harrison after working out in Fayetteville, Arkansas. He was going home to take his mother to church, when his car went left of center and was hit head on by a semi-truck. He didn't make it. He was only 22 years old.

Everyone in Harrison, Fayetteville, and Indianapolis were devastated by the loss. Brandon Burlsworth was in the prime of his life, and poised to be a solid pro football player for years to come. But months after he passed away, light shined through the darkness. Brandon's spirit was still with his loved ones. The Brandon Burlsworth Foundation was founded in the fall of 1999 to help underprivileged kids, which was something Brandon had planned to do during and after his professional football career.

A college football trophy was even named after him. The Brandon Burlsworth Trophy was established in 2010. The player who wins this award is recognized as the top football player in the country who started their college career as a walk-on. Notable players to win the award include Hunter Renfrow, Stetson Bennett, and Baker Mayfield.

You may be discouraged. You may have a dream that you want so badly that just seems so far away. Brandon Burlsworth probably felt that way too. But he never gave up on his dream. He went through the painful but rewarding process of putting in the work to make his dream a reality.

It wasn't always easy for him. And I'm sure there were days where he didn't have fun. But he never quit when most people probably would have. But he had the crazy dream of playing for his favorite football team as a child, and he did whatever it took to get there. He made that dream a reality and more.

Think about it: What's your "crazy dream"? What is the one thing you can't imagine not doing? Whatever that dream is, pursue it. Go after it with everything you have inside you. Put all your physical, mental, and spiritual strength into going after it. Brandon Burlsworth did that with his dream. And now he'll be remembered forever.

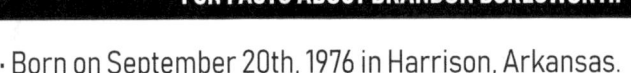

· Born on September 20th, 1976 in Harrison, Arkansas.

· Burlsworth's #77 is one of only two numbers retired by the Arkansas football program. The other number is #12, Clyde Scott.

· Burlsworth's story is retold in the 2016 movie, *Greater*.

· He was the first player in Arkansas history to complete his Master's Degree before playing his final college game.

· He was posthumously inducted into the Arkansas Sports Hall of Fame in 2002.

· Selected 63rd overall by the Colts in the 1999 NFL Draft.

· Had zero Division I scholarship offers.

· Was a devout Christian. This shaped every aspect of his life.

· Would have helped children and the less fortunate after his retirement from football if he had lived. This became the beginning of the Brandon Burlsworth Foundation.

· His locker is encased and preserved in his honor to this very day.

1. What was Brandon Burlsworth's number in college?

2. What position did he play?

3. True or false: The movie based on his life is called *The Brandon Burlsworth Story*.

4. True or false: There is also a book based on his life.

5. True or false: There is a college football award named in his honor.

6. True or false: The Colts retired Brandon Burlsworth's number.

7. True or false: The Brandon Burlsworth Foundation awards 19 different scholarships in his honor.

8. True or false: 90% of the families served by the foundation were families in need.

9. True or false: The foundation is still run by Burlsworth's family, even though he's gone.

10. True or false: Arkansas football still honors Brandon's memory every season.

ANSWER

1. 77.
2. Offensive guard
3. False. The movie is simply called *Greater* and was released in 2016.
4. True. It's called *Through the Eyes of a Champion: The Brandon Burlsworth Story.*
5. True. The Burlsworth Trophy is given in his honor, to the most outstanding Division I college football player who began their career as a walk-on, just like Brandon did.
6. False. The number was already retired in honor of Hall of Famer Jim Parker, but the team did feature Burlsworth on page 77 of their media guide.
7. True! Every year, the foundation awards 18 $5,000 scholarships and one $10,000 athletic scholarship.
8. False. 96% of the families were families served by the foundation are families in need, which shows that Brandon's memory is truly being honored by helping others.
9. True. Brandon's older brother Marty is the President of the foundation, and is still very active in honoring his brother's memory.
10. True! The team still encourages their players to "Do it the Burls Way" which means showing up early, leaving late, and giving 100 percent!

"Brandon was so single-minded, so focused. He didn't take one summer off the entire time he was at Arkansas. Other boys would go home after school got out in May and stay there until camp started in late July. But Brandon would stay on campus, working — painting the stadium, setting up dorms, things like that — and taking classes. So by his fourth year at Arkansas, he was already finishing his masters degree." -Marty Burlsworth

"Brandon's story is far more powerful than Rudy. He was and still is, my favorite Hog!" -Shane Perkins

"He did things to the end of the whistle. And he was always working, from the beginning to the end. His body, he had good bend and his size was appropriate. I was like, 'Holy cow, I really like this guy.'" -Howard Mudd

"Arkansas was the dream. And if Brandon was doing whatever he could on the field, then I sure as heck would do whatever I could to help get my brother there." -Marty Burlsworth

"Brandon belonged on that field, and he knew it. He was a Razorback. Some of his teammates have since told me how red his face would be during practice, how hard he went, how he never gave up." -Marty Burlsworth

LESSONS FROM STORY

· Achieving dreams takes hard work and a great work ethic.

· Faith in yourself, your abilities, and God can move mountains.

· Focus on one day at a time. Your dreams won't be achieved overnight.

· Work so hard that your friends and family are inspired by your example.

· Show up early and stay late if you want to make your dreams happen.

CRIS CARTER

THE WINDING ROAD TO CANTON

Struggles are a natural part of being human. It's part of life. From the average person to the richest person in the world, everybody has to overcome some kind of struggle on their way to success. Cris Carter did too. But unlike most people's path to greatness, Carter didn't experience his first taste of success and stay there. He reached the top, and then failed not once, but twice. And he still had the strength and the willpower to rebound to become a good person, and one of the greatest NFL wide receivers of all time. This is his story.

Cris Carter was born on November 25, 1965, in Troy, Ohio, and was one of seven children. When Cris was young, his mother moved him and his siblings to Middletown, Ohio, near Cincinnati. It was here that Cris first realized that he had tremendous talent as an athlete in both football and basketball. He was a star player in both sports for Middletown High School.

Cris's initial dream was to play in the NBA. But not for the reason you might think. Of course he wanted to make it big, and make his mark on the world, But he didn't really have a father in his life when he was a young boy. His dad left the family when he was very little. So he idolized his older brother Butch, who was an amazing athlete. He was so good in fact, that he played in the NBA for six seasons from 1980 to 1985 for the Lakers, Pacers, Knicks, and 76ers. Cris respected his brother greatly growing up. Butch was always there to give Cris advice both on and off the field and court.

The greatest piece of advice that Butch ever gave to Cris, came when Cris was starting to become locally famous as an athlete. Butch warned Cris to stay away from a place nicknamed "Hood's Corner." Hood's corner was the intersection of Sixteenth Avenue and Minnesota Street, and was an infamous spot in Middletown where many promising young athletes had fallen into crime and drugs. The older Carter brother gave his younger brother a stern warning: "I gave him six names, and I said, 'When we get to Hood's Corner, I guarantee you five of them will be there.' When we got there, five of them were there, and the sixth one was in jail. Cris said, 'Why did you give me those names?' And I said, 'These were the guys that were on this corner when I left to go to college.'" Butch Carter wanted his little brother to do better.

Butch played college basketball at Indiana University. But when it came time for Cris to choose where and how to continue his athletic career, he didn't choose to play basketball, but chose football instead. Ohio State head football coach Earle Bruce saw the potential Cris had as a star wide receiver, and convinced Carter to stay in his home state and play college football for the Ohio State Buckeyes, one of the most decorated college football programs in history.

Coach Bruce was absolutely right about Cris's talent. He could catch anything and everything. If it was a routine catch, he got it. If it was a one-handed catch, he got it. If it was an acrobatic midair catch, and he had to drag his feet to stay inbounds or score a touchdown? He almost always came down with it. There was nobody better at catching the football in the entire country than Cris Carter!

In three seasons as a Buckeye from 1984 to 1986, Cris caught 164 passes, 2,725 yards and 27 touchdowns. He was the most reliable receiver in all of college football while he was in Columbus. But before he had a chance to rewrite the record books in what could've been a Heisman-worthy senior season, Cris got in trouble. Serious trouble.

Cris may have been a fantastic wide receiver, but his entire family was still struggling with poverty. So he signed with an agent in an attempt to make a little money before going pro. Not only was signing with an agent illegal for college football players, but the agent that Cris signed with had connections to organized crime. Once everything came to light, Cris was suspended for his entire senior season. He was done. He never played another game of college football for Ohio State.

Before this mistake, his road to the NFL was set to be a cakewalk. He was so talented that he was projected to be a first-round pick. Now? It was like he didn't exist anymore. Teams refused to draft him. He wasn't even selected in the regular NFL Draft, and had to wait to be taken in the supplemental draft later by the Philadelphia Eagles.

Cris largely continued where he had left off in college. In his second season in the NFL in 1988, he caught 39 passes for 761 yards and six touchdowns. He followed that up in 1989 with 45 catches for 605 yards and 11 touchdowns. But just when it looked like his career was finally ready to take flight, the thing his brother Butch warned him about nearly ended his time as a pro football player: Cris really struggled with drugs.

Eagles coach Buddy Ryan ended up cutting Cris Carter from the team after the 1989 season. While it might have seemed like rock bottom for him at the time, getting cut was the best thing that could have happened to Cris. It was his wakeup call. Cris probably thought he had blown his chance to be an NFL player. But when the Minnesota Vikings claimed him for just $100, he took his next chance and ran with it. He never got in trouble again, focused intensely on being the best player and person he could be, and just did what he knew how to do best—catch the football. He also became a father for the first time soon after that, when his wife gave birth to their son, Duron Carter in 1991.

With a supportive and loving family in his corner, and a new lease on life in the NFL, Cris Carter was ready to revive his football career. As a Minnesota Viking, he had three solid seasons before he kicked it up several notches. From 1993 to 2000, Cris made the Pro Bowl eight straight times, and had five straight years of catching 10 touchdowns or more per season from 1995 to 1999. The bubbly but troubled kid from Middletown, Ohio, had beaten his demons. But even after he retired in 2002 after one season with the Miami Dolphins, football's highest honor remained out of his reach.

When the best NFL players retire, they usually have to wait a minimum of five years before they're inducted into the Pro Football Hall of Fame in Canton, Ohio. But for many years after his eligibility began, Cris had to wait. And wait. And wait some more. He had done everything he possibly could to prove he belonged in pro football's most sacred place. Every year he missed out, he cried. It broke his heart. He didn't know what else he could have done to make it. The call never came.

Until 2013. That year, at 48 years old, Cris Carter was finally elected to the Pro Football Hall of Fame. After all his struggles to get out of poverty and beat his own issues, the NFL recognized him as one of its very best. Cris was emotional as he struggled to hold back tears on stage during his induction speech. But he remembered the end of his time with the Eagles, and thanked his former coach Buddy Ryan for pushing him toward where he now stood.

"Buddy Ryan drafted me. He tried to grow me up in the league. And actually what Buddy Ryan did was the best thing that ever happened for me, when he cut me, and told me I couldn't play for his football team. But he told me a story. He told me the night before, he went home and talked to his wife. And he asked his wife what he should do. And his wife told him, 'Don't cut Cris Carter. He's going to do something special with his life.' So Buddy Ryan, and your lovely wife, I thank you. You're going into the Hall with me tonight."

No matter if you have failed somewhere, or if you are struggling in or out of school, you have the chance to do something special with your life. It's never too late to make something happen. Cris Carter's story is proof that anyone can succeed and push themselves to greater heights than they ever thought possible!

· Born in Troy, Ohio on November 25th, 1965.

· 8x Pro Bowler (1993-2000).

· NFL Receptions Leader in 1994

· 3x NFL Receiving Touchdowns Leader (1995, 1997, 1999)

· All-American while at Ohio State (1986)

· Has five siblings, including brothers Butch and John Carter

· Most well-known as a wide receiver for the Minnesota Vikings.

· Inducted into the Pro Football Hall of Fame in 2013.

· Has two children, Duron and Monterae Carter.

· Worked as a football analyst for several different channels and companies.

TRIVIA QUESTIONS

1. What was Cris Carter's number when he played for the Vikings?

2. True or false: Cris Carter is the only athlete in his family.

3. True or false: Cris Carter won the Heisman Trophy in college.

4. True or false: Cris Carter got inducted into the Pro Football Hall of Fame on his first try.

5. True or false: Cris Carter was bought by the Vikings for $100.

6. True or False: Cris Carter was the first NFL player ever to have a 150-yard receiving game in three different decades.

7. True or false: He was a Pro Bowl wide receiver early in his career with the Eagles.

8. He says that being cut from the Eagles was the best thing to ever happen to him.

9. At the time of his retirement, he ranked second in career catches and touchdowns, only behind Jerry Rice.

10. True or false: He played for only two NFL teams, the Vikings and Eagles.

ANSWER

1. Cris Carter wore #80 for Minnesota. It has since been retired by the team.
2. False. Cris Carter's older brother Butch was an NBA player, and Cris's son, Duron Carter played college football at Ohio State.
3. False. Although he was a spectacular college football player at Ohio State, Cris Carter never won the Heisman Trophy.
4. False. It took him six years and five tries before he finally made it in.
5. True. The team bought the rights to him for a measly $100 after he was cut by the Eagles.
6. True! He even beat out Jerry Rice, who was the second player to do it.
7. False.
8. True.
9. True.
10. False. He ended his career with the Miami Dolphins.

QUOTES FROM CRIS CARTER:

"Your image in sports will always matter."

"It's an unbelievably tough process. And there ain't no bums in the Hall. I mean, they're putting in great players every year."

"The difference between the good players and the great players is how long they stay in their prime."

"Football gave me a sense of purpose. It gave me a sense of me."

"I'm a competitor at the highest level. I like to compete."

LESSONS FROM STORY

• Listen to your parents and older siblings. They have advice that could save your life.

• Sometimes the best things to ever happen to you will be failures in life. Learn from them and use them for success later on.

• When you learn and grow, teach the younger ones what you know. Pass it on. Be a mentor to them.

• If you have a dream, never stop working for it. Fight through failures.

• Stay humble, even when you're on top. Don't forget what it took to get there.

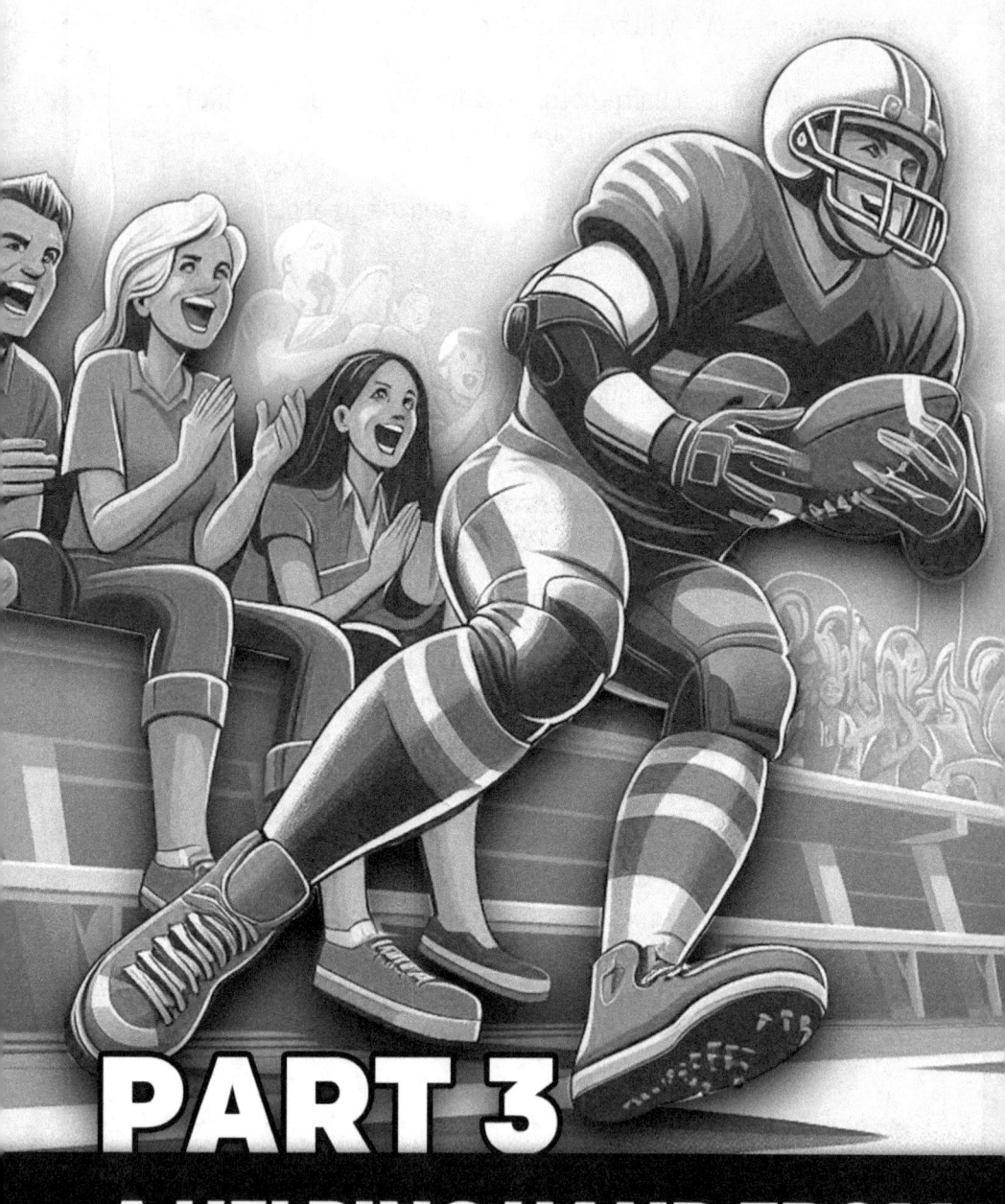

PART 3

A HELPING HAND FROM FAMILY AND FRIENDS

RAIDERS VS. TEXANS

THIS ONE IS FOR AL

On October 8, 2011, the football world lost one of its most unique and legendary people. Oakland Raiders owner Al Davis passed away at the age of 82. In his time as Raiders owner from 1972 to 2011, Davis was quite the character, and was known for many things. From his slicked back hair, trademark dark sunglasses, intensity as an owner, and his unwavering dedication to his team, Al was a Raider through and through.

Al wasn't afraid to do things a little differently either. This could mean encouraging his coaches to play more aggressively to catch opponents by surprise. Or it could mean going head-to-head with the NFL when he or his team was being mistreated or disrespected. He feared absolutely no one. But above all, Al Davis had a determination to be a winner and lead a bunch of winners. That was the most important thing in the world to him during his life. And it showed. For a stretch in the 1970s and

1980s, the Raiders were one of the most successful teams not just in the NFL, but in all of sports. From 1972 to 1985, the team made the playoffs 11 times, won the AFC West seven times, and won three Super Bowls in 1976, 1980, and 1983.

Now with Al gone, the Raiders would not only have to move on without him, but they would also have to channel him as best as they could during their next game of the 2011 season against the Houston Texans. This meant that Oakland would have to play with a confident swagger, be extra aggressive, and steal chances to win the game with either hard-hitting defense or trick plays to catch Houston off guard. But for most of the first half, Oakland couldn't get anything going offensively, and had to settle for two field goals from All-Pro kicker Sebastian Janikowski. The Raiders were bottled up, down 14-6, and Houston was threatening to spoil Oakland's effort to honor their late owner.

However, the Texans got too aggressive with just over a minute to go before halftime. They came after Raiders quarterback Jason Campbell by sending nearly all their defenders on a blitz to try and bring him down. He flipped the ball to wide receiver Darrius Heyward-Bey, who broke one tackle, made defenders miss on another, and sprinted 30 yards to the endzone! Touchdown! The Raiders had been outgunned, outplayed, and outgained all day long. But the spirit of Al Davis was with them on that touchdown play.

After the Raiders scored, both defenses stiffened up as Oakland and Houston could only each manage a field goal. Houston led 17-15 late in the third quarter. Oakland still had a chance to win the game for Al. The defense played like they still had a chance to win. They gang tackled Houston running backs and receivers, swarmed to the football and delivered vicious hits. This team wasn't playing like a bunch of men who had just lost their boss and dear friend—they were playing inspired, passionate football. They were playing just like the Raider in their iconic team song, "The Autumn Wind":

The Autumn Wind is a pirate, blustering in from sea. With a rollicking song, he sweeps along, swaggering boisterously.

His face is weather-beaten. He wears a hooded sash. With a silver hat about his head. And a bristling black mustache.

He growls as he storms the country. A villain big and bold. And the trees all shake, and quiver and quake, as he robs them of their gold.

The Autumn Wind is a raider, pillaging just for fun. He'll knock you 'round and upside down, and laugh when he's conquered and won.

But for as well as the defense was playing, Oakland hadn't finished things off yet. They still trailed by a slim margin, and needed to break through somehow before they could even begin to think of celebrating for Al. After a great kickoff return by Jacoby Ford helped put the offense in decent position at their own 40-yard line, the Raiders began their march. Running back Darren McFadden put Oakland on his back that drive, as he ran the football with power, strength and authority. He either slipped through the fingers of Texans defenders, or bowled them over with punishing runs. Houston had no answer for him. There was no stopping him once he got rolling. He was both as slippery as a bar of soap, and as hard as a bowling ball!

Before long, the Raiders found themselves in prime position to score a go-ahead touchdown early in the fourth quarter. They were at Houston's 19-yard line. They were so close to snatching the lead. The opportunity was right there in front of them. And they were not going to let the chance slip through their fingers.

After Jason Campbell snapped the football, he fearlessly weaved through defenders and fired a perfect pass to wide receiver to Chaz Schilens, who was waiting by the left sideline. Once Schilens grabbed the football, he scampered into the endzone! Touchdown! After the touchdown, both defenses buckled down and only allowed a field goal each. But Oakland still led the game. They were almost home. They led the Texans 25-20. But they still had under two minutes left to hold the lead.

Could they do it? Could the Raiders finish the game, and win one for their beloved owner and friend, Al Davis? Or would they choke at the last minute? Texans quarterback Matt Schaub began to march Houston down the field. He was cool, calm, and collected. Nothing was bothering him. And he was poised to break the hearts of Raider fans everywhere.

The Texans moved all the way down to Oakland's 39-yard line. And with just 29 seconds left on the clock, Schaub fired a deep bomb to tight end Joel Dreessen, who snagged the ball at the Raiders five-yard line. Oh no. Here it was. After going through heartache the day before, the Raiders were going to feel it all over again. They were going to choke this one away. Matt Schaub ran the clock all the way down to eight seconds left before spiking the football. Houston was eight seconds away from a stunning victory.

Schaub brought the Texans offense out of the huddle. As he was surveying the field, he saw the perfect matchup he wanted and snapped the football to start the final play of the game. Schaub saw an open running lane and took off for the endzone. But he was contained by the Raider defense and nearly forced out of bounds. He threw the football back across the field in the other direction hoping one of his receivers would catch it. But Raiders safety Michael Huff snatched the ball out of the air and fell to the ground. Interception! Ballgame! RAIDERS WIN!

This team had lost one of the most iconic owners in sports just 24 hours before this game. But to them, he was so much more. Al Davis was their boss, teacher, good friend and biggest supporter. They finished this one for him. They beat Houston in an ugly game. But as Al was fond of saying: "Just win, baby." The win over Houston wasn't stylish or flashy. It wasn't a walk in the park either. But it fit the way Oakland played football. It was a true Raider victory.

After the game in an ecstatic locker room, several men were crying their eyes out. Head coach Hue Jackson was crying as well. As he was trying to hold back tears, Jackson told reporters that he felt that Al Davis's spirit was with him on the sidelines during the game. "One thing Al always taught me was he said: 'Hue don't believe in plays, believe in players and eventually the players will make plays for you,'" Jackson said. "And that's what I did. I could just hear him saying that to me the whole time. Believe in your players and not the plays."

The Raiders believed in themselves even when their hearts were heavy, and they were hurting more than anyone could have imagined. But they fought and won for the man who had believed in them. They won for Al. There will be times in life where you are hurting more than anyone can know. Whether it's from struggling in life, or losing someone dear to you. But they would want you to continue. The Raiders honored Al Davis by winning the game for him.

You can honor your departed loved ones too. Perhaps your grandma loved gardening or cooking big meals for you and the family. Or maybe your grandpa loved working with his hands and building things for you. Whatever your family members or friends enjoyed doing, taking part in it honors them and makes them proud. They're smiling down on you and watching over you whenever you honor them and remember the impact that they had on you!

· Al Davis was Jewish.

· Al Davis was extremely persuasive, and able to talk his way into, or out of any situation. He was smart and incredibly witty.

· Al Davis played both football and basketball in his younger days. He wasn't the most talented player, but he never gave up. He was really scrappy and he played hard.

· He was a big supporter of Civil Rights. He refused to led the Raiders play in any city where the players were still segregated.

· Owned the Raiders for 39 years, from 1972 to 2011.

· Ownership has stayed in Al's family, as his son Mark Davis currently owns the team.

· Al was born in Brockton, Massachusetts in 1929.

· Graduated from Syracuse University in Syracuse, New York in 1950.

· "Just win, baby" is Al's famous phrase.

· Often wore all black and sunglasses.

1. True or False: Al Davis was a seasoned coach when he landed his first job in the pros.

2. True or False Under Al, the Raiders won three Super Bowls.

3. True or False: Al was named AFL Coach of the Year in his first season coaching the Raiders in 1963.

4. True or False: Al Davis never moved the Raiders during his ownership.

5. True or False: Al Davis was inducted into the Pro Football Hall of Fame in 1992.

6. True or False: He coached a U.S. Army football team in the early 1950's.

7. True or False: He once sued the NFL.

8. True or False: Al was a high school and college football star.

9. True or False: Al Davis had a winning record as a professional football coach before taking over as Raiders owner.

10. True or False: Al Davis is the only person in football history to serve as an assistant coach, head coach, general manager, owner and commissioner.

ANSWER

1. False. Even though he's now known as a successful NFL owner, Al had zero coaching experience when he started.
2. True. The Raiders won Super Bowls in 1976, 1980 and 1983.
3. True! The team went 1-13 in 1962, and turned around and went 10-4 under Al's leadership in 1963.
4. False. He moved the team twice because he was unhappy with both stadiums.
5. True.
6. True.
7. True.
8. False. He never was known for any athletic ability. But he had a keen football mind, and loved strategy.
9. True! He went 23-16-3 as Raiders head coach.
10. True!

"The fire that burns brightest in the Raiders organization is the will to win."

"We would rather be feared than respected."

"I had a dream that someday I would build the finest organization in professional sports."

"We all know that time never really stops for the great ones. It reaches out and wraps them in a cloak of immortality."

"Aside from my will to win, my commitment to excellence, the fire that burns brightest in me is the great love and enthusiasm that I have and had for the game of football and for everyone and everything connected with it. I love the game; I love the league; I love my team."

LESSONS FROM STORY

· Fight through adversity. The Raiders lost Al, but they didn't quit. Don't quit in spite of loss, either.

· Honor your loved ones who have passed away. The Raiders honored Al by winning the first game for him after he died.

· Be true to who you are. Al Davis didn't change who he was for anyone, and people loved him for it.

· Fear no one.

· If you have a dream, go for it. Al was never a football star. But he dreamed he would build a winning organization. He did it. You can achieve your dreams too!

JIMMY GRAHAM

THE POWER OF FAMILY

If you have loving parents, hug them always. If you have a father who gives you life advice because he cares about you, let him know how much you appreciate him and his wisdom. If you have a loving mother who nurtures you, helps you grow into a decent person, and is there for you in good times and bad, let her know how much she means to you.

Jimmy Graham, a Pro Bowl tight end for the New Orleans Saints, didn't have any of that growing up. Not even close. He was born in Goldsboro, North Carolina, to a financially unstable woman who had no business raising him. When Jimmy was an 11-year-old kid, she abandoned him at a group home. Things didn't get any better for him there, as he was relentlessly bullied by older kids in the home. One day, he ran away from being bullied, neglected, and mistreated, and found his way to Abundant Life Fellowship Church. Jimmy was hungry, freezing cold, and had nowhere else to go. But these people showed him love for the first time in his life, took him in, and loved him as if he were one of their own family members.

Then, while he was with the prayer group one day, Jimmy broke down and told them through tears what he had been through. This touched everyone in the group and at the church. But the person Jimmy touched the most through his story, was a woman named Becky Vinson, the woman who would eventually become his mother. She heard Jimmy's story and decided to adopt him as her son. She couldn't just leave him there by himself. "How do you hear something like that, and then go home?" she said in an interview years later. "I'm not that person. That's not me. I just can't do that. I told him, 'We can talk to your mom. You can come stay with me.'"

Becky already had a daughter, Karina, and was putting herself through nursing school. She didn't have a lot of money at the time. But Jimmy didn't care. He had the family he always wanted. It didn't matter that they were living in a trailer. He had people who loved him, and he loved them back. Once Becky got a nursing job, the family was finally in a better financial situation. Jimmy saw how hard his mother worked to make life better for him and his sister Karina. And that inspired him to improve his grades, care about school, and care about doing his best.

He soon became a student who regularly earned A's and B's on his report card. Not only that, he began playing basketball at Charis Prep in Wilson, North Carolina. He did so well in the classroom and on the hardwood, that the Miami Hurricanes eventually came calling. They offered Jimmy a full scholarship and he was all too happy to accept it!

For the first three years of his college career, Jimmy was an average basketball player. He averaged four points and four rebounds per game. But during his senior season in 2009, he would discover his talent and love for football. Jimmy was enjoying his career as a college athlete. But he knew that he could be getting more out of his time as a Miami Hurricane. As fate would have it, he eventually got in touch with Miami football legend Bernie Kosar.

Bernie Kosar is famous in South Florida for being the quarterback who led the Hurricanes to their first National Championship in 1983, and he has his own chapter later on in this book. Jimmy may have started out as a basketball player. But Kosar noticed his potential as a football player. When the two would spend time together sharpening the skills that Jimmy would need to play football, the former Pro Bowl quarterback was in awe of what he saw.

"He's got as good a pair of hands as anybody I've thrown to. And I've played in AFC Championship games. Then I started talking about routes, and he seemed to pick it up," Kosar said. And with that physical presence and the way he uses his body, I could throw it 11 feet in the air, and he'd still jump up 12 feet to get it."

Not only did Bernie Kosar notice Jimmy's talent, he also believed in his ability to use it to make something of himself. Becky loved him enough to adopt him. And now a wise mentor, Bernie, believed enough in Jimmy's potential to help push him toward greatness. "I kept telling him, 'Jimmy, not only are you going to be a great player, you're going to be a superstar,' Kosar said. "He looked at me like I was an idiot or trying to be nice. But I just believed it from the first time I threw to him."

Jimmy played in every single game for Miami during the 2009 season. He didn't get a lot of catches that year. He only snagged 17 catches in 13 games. But he managed to rack up 213 yards and five receiving touchdowns as a tight end. A tight end is a player who is big enough to block like a lineman, but they're fast enough to catch passes like a receiver, and they're reliable enough for a quarterback to throw to if the team is close to scoring a touchdown.

Jimmy showed off enough talent to catch the eye of the New Orleans Saints, and the team took him in the third round of the 2010 NFL Draft with the 95th overall pick. Jimmy Graham was once a neglected, unloved, unwanted boy from Goldsboro, North Carolina. And now he stood at the doorstep of making a living for himself as an NFL player. He had come so far. But he wasn't done yet!

Through the first four years of his career, Jimmy Graham was counted on to make big-time plays for the Saints. Since he's 6'7 and 265 pounds, quarterback Drew Brees often threw to Graham when nobody else was open because he was tall enough to leap up and grab the football. This is where Graham's basketball background came in handy. But not only did he play extremely well, he also set some Saints records in the process. In 2011, he became the first Saints tight end to have over 1,000 receiving yards in a season, and tied the Saints record for most catches in a season with 99.

After 2014, Jimmy bounced around the league, and spent time with the Seahawks, Packers, and Bears. He was consistent and reliable, but wasn't quite as explosive as he had been at the start of his career. But he eventually came back to New Orleans in 2023. He now has a chance to finish his career in the place where it all started.

The Saints were the first ones to give him a shot. They were the first ones to give the kid from Goldsboro, North Carolina a chance to live his dream. And even though he's now in his later thirties and a veteran NFL player, he might still have more left in the tank. But even before Jimmy had a chance to live his dream, it all began thanks to love and care from other people. God guided Jimmy to his mom, Becky Vinson, sister Karina Vinson, and Bernie Kosar. They were at least three people who loved Jimmy enough and believed in him enough to help him get on his feet, and encouraged him to live out his best life.

Who are the people in your life who have always been in your corner? Think about them for a second. Maybe they're your parents, grandparents, aunts, uncles, classmates, teachers, or friends. But if anyone has seen something special in you, and they've nurtured you and encouraged you as you've grown up, thank them. Tell them how much they mean to you. And honor what they did for you by trying your best to succeed in whatever you do. When you do that, you're mirroring what Jimmy Graham does for his mom, sister, Bernie Kosar, and everyone else who believed in him.

While you should always believe in yourself, it's important to have a support system full of family, friends, and other loved ones. They can help you reach new heights that you never thought were possible!

· Born November 24th, 1986 in Goldsboro, Carolina.

· Survived a difficult upbringing before he was adopted by his real mom, Becky Vinson.

· He was a basketball star before he ever became a star in football.

· Played both sports for the University of Miami Hurricanes.

· Friends with former NFL star quarterback Bernie Kosar.

· Led the NFL in receiving touchdowns in 2013 as a tight end.

· Stands 6'7 and weighs 265 pounds.

· Runs his own foundation, The Jimmy Graham Foundation, which helps military veterans and at-risk kids.

· He's an avid pilot in his spare time.

· He was nominated as the Walter Payton Man of the Year, which is an award for the NFL player who helps the most with charity and philanthropy.

1. True or False: Jimmy Graham finished his college degree while at Miami.

2. How many career touchdowns does Jimmy Graham have?

3. How many teams has Jimmy Graham played for in the NFL?

4. True or False: Jimmy Graham was taken in the first round of the NFL Draft.

5. True or False: Jimmy Graham caught his first NFL touchdown in his home state of North Carolina.

6. True or False: Jimmy Graham has been named a Pro Bowler twice.

7. True or False: Jimmy Graham has over 700 career receptions.

8. True or False: Jimmy Graham has 10 100-yard receiving games.

9. True or False: His career high in receiving yards is 179.

10. True or False: He was once hit by a car, but did more damage to the car than it did to him.

ANSWER

1. True. He finished college with a double major in marketing and management, all while playing football.
2. Jimmy Graham has 89 career receiving touchdowns.
3. Four. He's played for the Saints, Packers, Bears and Seahawks.
4. False. He was taken in the third round of the NFL Draft, #95 overall.
5. True! He caught his first touchdown against the Carolina Panthers.
6. False. Jimmy Graham has been named a Pro Bowler five times.
7. True. He has 719 career receptions
8. False. He has 19 career 100-yard receiving games.
9. True.
10. True.

QUOTES FROM JIMMY GRAHAM

"The best way to motivate me, is to tell me I can't do something."

"I played college basketball. When I first decided I was going to play football, there were a lot of people telling me that I wasn't going to make it."

"In my life, there have been a lot of people who weren't there for me. So to now have people counting on me is awesome."

"The first four years of my career, I never complained. I never demanded. I never said anything about money."

"I don't have chips on my shoulders. I have bricks."

LESSONS FROM STORY

· Appreciate your parents if you have them in your life.

· A good father or mother figure in your life can make all the difference.

· The hardest workers usually come from nothing.

· Education is important. It is one of the keys to your success in life.

· Never forget where you came from even if you make it to the top.

LADAINIAN TOMLINSON

ACTIONS SPEAK LOUDER THAN WORDS

Some athletes are really cocky. They're extremely talented, and they know it. They also often tell everyone how great they are. They're all over social media, TV, and in the spotlight. Former Chargers running back LaDainian Tomlinson, commonly known as "LT," is different. He's the exact opposite. The native of Rosebud, Texas, has always preferred to stay humble in every area of his life. But there was no denying that LaDainian had a special gift for playing football. And this was clear even from the time he was a little boy.

His passion for the sport grew from an early age thanks to a little game he played with his father, Oliver Tomlinson. Sundays in the early to mid-1980s in the Tomlinson house were spent watching football. Often, Oliver would get up to leave the room to do household chores and leave LaDainian by himself to watch the game for a few minutes. But when Oliver returned, he would quiz his son on what had happened during that part of the football game. LaDainian quickly learned the rules of the game, the positions, and the strategy that was a part of the sport. He also quickly became a fan of the best players. And one player would shape who he would become, not just as a football player, but as a person.

Walter Payton, nicknamed "Sweetness," was a Hall of Fame running back who played his entire career with the Chicago Bears from 1975 to 1987. He wasn't very big or tall for a football player. He only stood 5'10 and weighed 200 pounds, which is small for an NFL running back. But what Payton lacked in size, he made up for with speed, elusiveness, and power. He was extremely strong. Young LaDainian Tomlinson idolized Walter Payton and wanted to become like him. And after Payton retired from football, LT rooted for a similar running back in Emmitt Smith as he was growing up.

According to LaDainian's mother Loreane, her son was a quiet boy who hardly ever asked his mother for anything. So when he begged her to go to a Cowboys football camp, she gave in. She knew he was serious. "LaDainian is one of those rare kids, that he doesn't ask for anything," she said. "So when you look at him asking and he's so joyful about it, he's going to work every way possible to do everything he can to get that dream."

At the camp, Cowboys players were helping kids go through all kinds of drills. Handling handoffs for running back drills, was none other than LaDainian's idol, Emmitt Smith. LT could hardly believe his eyes! He was next in line to take a handoff from Smith and show off his running skills, even as dozens of other boys crowded behind him, trying to get the handoff first. But LT not only took the handoff from Smith, he impressed the Cowboys legend. "He was one of those kids that you just cannot ignore," Smith said. "He's one of those kids where you sit back, and you're like 'Wow. You keep it up, you're going to be something someday.'"

LaDainian took Emmitt Smith's approval and ran with it. Literally. Once he got the chance to make some big-time plays on the football field, he never looked back. In the first game of his senior year at University High School, LT scored not one, not two, but six touchdowns! He was determined to make his football dreams come true. He even predicted his own future. In a letter to his mother, LT let his mom know just how much he appreciated her, and promised her he would make it big:

Hello Mom,

How are you doing? Mom, I love you so much that every time I say it or write it, it brings tears to my eyes. One day you will be the proudest mom in the world, because I am going to go to college and graduate. And if God is willing, go on to play pro football and be the best person I can, because that's how you raised me.

Mom, I thank you so much for everything you have, and are still doing for me, because it's hard not having a father who I can talk to and get advice from. You did the very best.

Love, LaDainian.

LT went to the only school that would offer him a scholarship, Texas Christian University, and he stuffed the stat sheet. During his four seasons with the Horned Frogs from 1997 to 2000, he ran for over 5,600 yards and scored 54 rushing touchdowns.

Not only that, LT also set the all-time NCAA record for yards in a game, when he absolutely shredded UTEP for 406 yards and six touchdowns! This was enough to catch the eye of the Chargers, who took Tomlinson with the 5th overall pick in the 2001 NFL Draft.

LT would soon become a superstar in San Diego. He won the MVP in 2006, and set the record for most touchdowns scored in a season with 31. But for as electrifying as he was, the chance to win a Super Bowl unfortunately eluded him. He was on several playoff teams, and had won AFC West titles, but he couldn't quite get over the hump. And after five Pro Bowl appearances for the Chargers, a knee injury would signal the end of his time in San Diego.

In an emotional press conference, LT was crying as he said goodbye to the place that had been his home for nine years: "Sometimes emotions is what makes a person. And as you guys know, I've always worn my emotions on my sleeve. So for that I'm not sorry. And I thank you."

He had wanted nothing more than to bring a Super Bowl Championship to San Diego for Chargers fans. He loved his adopted home city with all his heart. And not being able to do it for them just about broke him. But surprisingly after he signed on with the New York Jets, LT was revived. The Chargers had moved away from being a running team, while the Jets under head coach Rex Ryan, loved to run the football.

The year 2010 was LT's best season as a Jet, where he ran for 914 yards and six touchdowns. And he also was a key piece of a team that finally helped him get revenge on the team that had haunted him for so long when he was still a Charger: The New England Patriots. When LT was still in San Diego, the Chargers had some truly great teams. But every single time they dared to take that big step toward appearing in the Super Bowl, Tom Brady and his teammates always managed to win. The Patriots defeated the Chargers four straight times in the playoffs.

Not this time. The Jets defeated the Patriots in the AFC Divisional Round 28-21 and sent them packing! The Jets came to the brink of appearing in their second Super Bowl in franchise history, but unfortunately lost 24-19 to the Pittsburgh Steelers in the AFC Championship Game. But by this point in his career, LT was at peace with where he was. Yes, he wanted desperately to win a Super Bowl with both the Chargers and Jets.

But something one of his old coaches once said, gave him a new perspective. Marty Schottenheimer, LaDainian's longtime coach in San Diego, reminded him of what was truly important in life. LT considered Schottenheimer a father figure throughout much of his career and had incredible respect for him. Marty's words still resonate with him to this day: "LT, there were many days that you had, that your friends had, and that your family, had, that were championship days," Coach Schottenheimer said. "Just because you didn't win the ultimate Super Bowl Championship, I know we have many memories that we can still call championship days."

Giving it your all. Making memories. Being there for your family, friends, and teammates. Staying humble in spite of success, and hopeful even after defeat. These are the things that matter most. Never give anything less than your best effort. But when you do fall short of your goals and dreams in life, don't beat yourself up. Just pick yourself up, dust yourself off and keep going. And when you do succeed and make it to the top in whatever you do, don't forget the people who were with you when you started at the bottom.

LaDainian Tomlinson started out just as a football-loving kid in a small town in eastern Texas. But even through the tough times in his life and career, he never gave up, he never forgot where he came from, and was always grateful to those who had helped him achieve his dream. He kept his promise to his mother. And he eventually became a Pro Football Hall of Famer in 2017. He stayed humble, hardworking, and never gave up. If you approach your life in the same way, success will come!

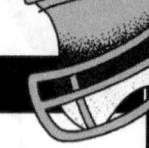

· Born on June 23rd, 1979 in Rosebud, Texas.

· Is Texas Christian University's all-time leading rusher.

· Finished fourth in the Heisman Trophy voting in college.

· He's 5'10 and 220 pounds.

· LaDainian Tomlinson scored 481.1 points in fantasy football in 2006. That is currently the greatest season in fantasy football history for any player.

· He has been married to his wife LaTorsha since 2003. They have two children.

· Along with football, LaDainian has also appeared in a few movies as an actor. He played a pastor in the 2018 Christian film *God Bless the Broken Road*.

· He is descended from slaves who lived in a place called Tomlinson Hill, Texas.

· He was named NFL MVP in 2006.

· Ran with both speed and power, in spite of being considered small for a running back.

1. True or False: He is in both the College Football Hall of Fame and the Pro Football Hall of Fame.

2. How many yards did LT rush for in his best college football game?

3. True or False: LT was picked in the third round of the NFL Draft, because people didn't respect him.

4. True or False: LaDainian Tomlinson once ran, threw for, and caught a touchdown in a single game.

5. True or False: LaDainian Tomlinson reached the 100-touchdown mark faster than anyone in NFL history.

6. True or False: He was a high school football star, and received several Division I college offers.

7. How many career rushing touchdowns does LT have?

8. True or False: He briefly played for the Saints with Drew Brees.

9. Who was LaDainian Tomlinson's idol growing up?

10. True or False: He met Emmitt Smith as a kid at a football camp.

ANSWER

1. True.
2. 406 yards. That's still an NCAA record! But broke by Melvin Gordon in 2014, who did 408 yards.
3. False. He was taken fifth overall in the 2001 NFL Draft.
4. True!
5. True. He did it in just 89 games!
6. False. People mostly overlooked him.
7. 145 rushing touchdowns.
8. False. Although Drew Brees and LT did play together in San Diego for the Chargers before Brees signed with New Orleans.
9. He had several idols growing up, but his favorites were Jim Brown, Emmitt Smith and Walter Payton..
10. True!

QUOTES FROM LADAINIAN TOMLINSON

"As long as you believe in Him, no matter what happens in your life, understand that it's all for a purpose."

"You know who your friends are at your lowest point."

"You earn the respect of your peers that you play against when they don't trash talk you."

"Sometimes when you're praised about something, sometimes it's deserved, and sometimes it's not deserved. Same thing with criticism. Sometimes the criticism is deserved, and sometimes it's not deserved."

"I make sure I always give Him all the glory and praise, because I know that in one second, one game, one play, it could be all over."

LESSONS FROM STORY

· If you have a special gift, cultivate it.

· Sometimes life doesn't make sense. Continue working hard and having faith in God anyway.

· Appreciate the sacrifices your parents make for you.

· Don't demand things from your parents. Be humble and quiet.

· It's okay to wear your emotions on your sleeve. It shows that you care.

JEROME BETTIS

HONORING THE FAMILY NAME

When he was raising his son in Detroit, Johnnie Bettis gave Jerome a simple command: Honor the family. He said, "Son, I can't give you much. But I have one thing I can give you: A good name. So don't screw it up." That one statement would guide Jerome Bettis for the rest of his life. That piece of advice from his father would serve as his compass both on and off the field. While he's now fondly known as a Hall of Famer, and a Super Bowl Champion running back, there was once a time where he almost didn't take the path that history had laid out for him.

Growing up as the oldest of three kids born to Johnnie and Gladys Bettis in Detroit, Michigan, Jerome learned firsthand what it was like to have to struggle, claw and fight just to make ends meet. Johnnie and Gladys were struggling financially and had a hard time raising their children in the 1980s. So Jerome and his brother took to the streets.

"The mindset was, we're in the hood, mom and dad are working their butts off, there's no money around and we need to make some money," he said. "So we said, you know what, let's give it a shot. It was one of those moments you regret. But at the moment, that was the only thing that was really available to us. That's the disheartening part of it all, is that here you had two young men and this was the opportunity that was available. So we took it. We took it and we sold drugs."

That was Jerome's brush with a darker path in life. But his mother Gladys, a sweet but strong woman, set him straight right away. "My husband and I, we instilled right and wrong in those kids, and that is something you don't do," she said. "I talked until I was blue in the face, and my god, it worked. He stopped. I guess he knew it was wrong, I don't know. But it worked."

That was the course correction Jerome needed. After that fateful talk with his mother, he refocused and found what would soon become his passion in life: football. "It kind of struck a nerve to the point where I said, 'Okay, I am going to stop. I am going to give it all up, and I am going to pursue football as a dream," Jerome said.

Once he'd decided to turn away from hustling on the streets, Jerome jumped headfirst into being a football player. Once he did, he discovered he had an incredible natural ability for it. His high school coach, Bob Dozier, noticed Jerome's stout build and potential right away. He recalled the first time he met the future Hall of Famer. "I was sitting at my desk doing some paperwork, and I heard a knock on the door. 'Coach, my name is Jerome Bettis, and I want to play football for you.' I saw this kid who looked like a Black Superman. And my reply to his question was, 'Hell yes son. You can play for me.'"

Once Jerome took the field for the first time as a freshman at Mackenzie High School, he never looked back. He began developing his trademark bruising running style that would eventually earn him the nickname "The Bus." But he was also a great player at linebacker, too. Jerome's skills eventually caught the eye of Lou Holtz, who recruited him to play as a running back for the Notre Dame Fighting Irish in 1990!

Even though he was built almost like a tight end, Jerome had surprisingly good footwork and was incredibly fast for a bigger guy. He was only 5'11, but he weighed over 250 pounds. And every time defenders tried to tackle him, he was either agile enough to spin out of tackles, or strong enough to power through them and run defenders over on his way to a touchdown.

This became so common for Bettis in 1991, that he set the Notre Dame record for rushing touchdowns scored in a season with 20, a record that still stands to this day. Not only that, he scored three more touchdowns against the Florida Gators to help the Irish win the 1992 Sugar Bowl in one of his finest college games. But before long, it was time for The Bus to continue rolling along on his journey to greatness. Next stop? Los Angeles. The Rams took Jerome Bettis with the 10th overall pick in the 1993 NFL Draft.

After only five games in the league, Jerome earned the starting spot for the Rams. He racked up 1,429 rushing yards, which was second in the entire league on his way to the Offensive Rookie of the Year. He was also named to his first Pro Bowl, and was the only rookie named to that year's All-Pro Team. But after a solid second season in Los Angeles in 1994, a coaching change caused Bettis's workload as a running back to drop significantly in 1995. It got so bad for him, that he briefly considered quitting football altogether.

His mother Gladys says her son was considering even going back to Notre Dame as a student to finish his degree: "Jerome came home. He was thinking about not going back, getting out of football," she said. "He said 'I'm going back to school and making sure I have my degree, because I don't think football is going to be it for me.'" But as fate would have it, a trade to Pittsburgh during the 1996 NFL Draft got The Bus back in gear. He was a natural as a Steeler. Unlike Los Angeles, which was focused on an explosive passing offense, Pittsburgh was the exact opposite. Just like the town they called home, the Steelers were a tough, blue-collar football team. And they loved to run the football.

But even though the Steelers were incredibly successful in the 1990s and early 2000s, one thing eluded them: A Super Bowl Championship. They hadn't won one since 1979, and hadn't appeared in one since 1995. And by the time he was a household name in the Steel City, Jerome Bettis was in the twilight of his career. After a particularly devastating loss to the New England Patriots in the 2004 Playoffs, the 32-year-old running back seriously considered retirement. He had suffered so many postseason heartbreaks that he wasn't sure he had the emotional strength to make another run at a Championship. Coming up short again would break him.

But just like the trade to Pittsburgh back in 1996, life intervened again. He became a father for the very first time when his wife gave birth to a baby girl, Jada. That gave The Bus all the motivation he needed to kick it in gear one final time. Jerome was determined to not only play his absolute best for his newborn daughter, he was also determined to win a Championship for his family. Johnnie and Gladys Bettis, and his siblings John and Kimberly, had always been in his corner. 2005 would be the year he would win one for them.

Many people thought 2004 would be Pittsburgh's year. They went 15-1 and looked every bit like a Super Bowl team. But the 2005 team would be the one to get over the hump. They went 11-5 and became the first Wild Card team ever to win three straight playoff games when they beat the Bengals, Colts, and Broncos to get to Super Bowl 40!

And as luck would have it, that year's Super Bowl would be played in Jerome's hometown: Detroit, Michigan. At Ford Field, the Steeler defense would shut down the Seahawks, and Pittsburgh steadily ran the football and controlled the game until they won by a final score of 21-10. Jerome Bettis wasn't the MVP that day. That honor went to his teammate, receiver Hines Ward. But Bettis had finally capped off his career the way he always wanted to: as a World Champion. The Bus's journey had come full circle. But that wasn't his final stop. The final stop would be in Canton, Ohio, at the Pro Football Hall of Fame in 2015.

But Jerome did something greater than win a Super Bowl or be inducted into the Pro Football Hall of Fame. He had made good on his dad Johnnie's wish: he'd honored the family name. He didn't mess it up. Good and supportive families can push you to do your absolute best. Jerome's family didn't let him give up on his dream, even though there were times he wanted to.

No matter what your dream is, and no matter what kind of family you have, lean on them. Honor them by what you do. That could mean doing well in school, helping them out around the house, or taking care of them on bad days. But if they've been there for you in life, the best thing you can do is to pay back their kindness by being there for them!

· Jerome's brother John presented him for his Hall of Fame induction in 2015.

· Jerome Bettis Jr. is following in his dad's footsteps. He's committed to play football at Notre Dame.

· Jerome's mom Gladys is a cancer survivor. She's cancer-free after being diagnosed in 2015.

· Born in Detroit, Michigan on February 16th, 1972.

· Played college football for Notre Dame from 1990-1992.

· He set the Notre Dame record for touchdowns by one player in a season with 20, in 1991 during his junior season.

· He was named to the Pro Bowl six times.

· He is a member of the Pittsburgh Steelers All-Time Team, the Pittsburgh Steelers Hall of Honor, and the Pittsburgh Sports Hall of Fame.

· In 2022, 30 years after playing for the Fighting Irish, Jerome Bettis finally graduated from Notre Dame with a degree in Business.

· Was named the 1993 NFL Rookie of the Year with the Los Angeles Rams.

1. What number did Jerome Bettis wear in college for Notre Dame?

2. What number did Jerome Bettis wear in the pros?

3. Where does Jerome Bettis rank on the all-time rushing list?

4. How long did Jerome Bettis play in the NFL?

5. True or False: Jerome's nickname is "The Jackhammer."

6. True or False: He's a first-ballot Hall of Famer.

7. True or False: He was traded from the Rams to the Steelers on Draft Day, 1996.

8. True or False: He has asthma.

9. True or False: His son plays for Notre Dame.

10. True or False: He won three Super Bowls.

ANSWER

1. #6.
2. He wore #36 his whole career with both the Rams and Steelers.
3. He sits just outside the Top 5. He's sixth on the list with 13,662 rushing yards.
4. He played in the NFL for 13 seasons.
5. False. His nickname is "The Bus."
6. False. He didn't make it into the Hall of Fame until 2015.
7. True. He has 719 career receptions
8. True.
9. True. Jerome Bettis Jr. plays for the Fighting Irish just like his dad.
10. False. He won one Super Bowl, but it was extra special since he won it in his hometown of Detroit!

"My dad was my hero. The strongest man I'll ever know."

"I played this game to win a championship. I am a champion. I think the Bus's last stop is here in Detroit."

"You want bold? Ask the hundreds of defensive backs I ran over during my career if they think I'm bold."

"Fame is fleeting, and you can't get caught up in it. Signing autographs, taking pictures, and being nice to people is a small price to pay for the upside that comes with this."

"Just give me one more year. I'll get you that trophy."

LESSONS FROM STORY

· A supportive family can push you to goals you never thought possible.

· Do your best to honor your family name.

· Give credit to people when they pick you up and help you out.

· Life sometimes throws unexpected things at you. Roll with them.

· Be an unselfish team player in everything you do.

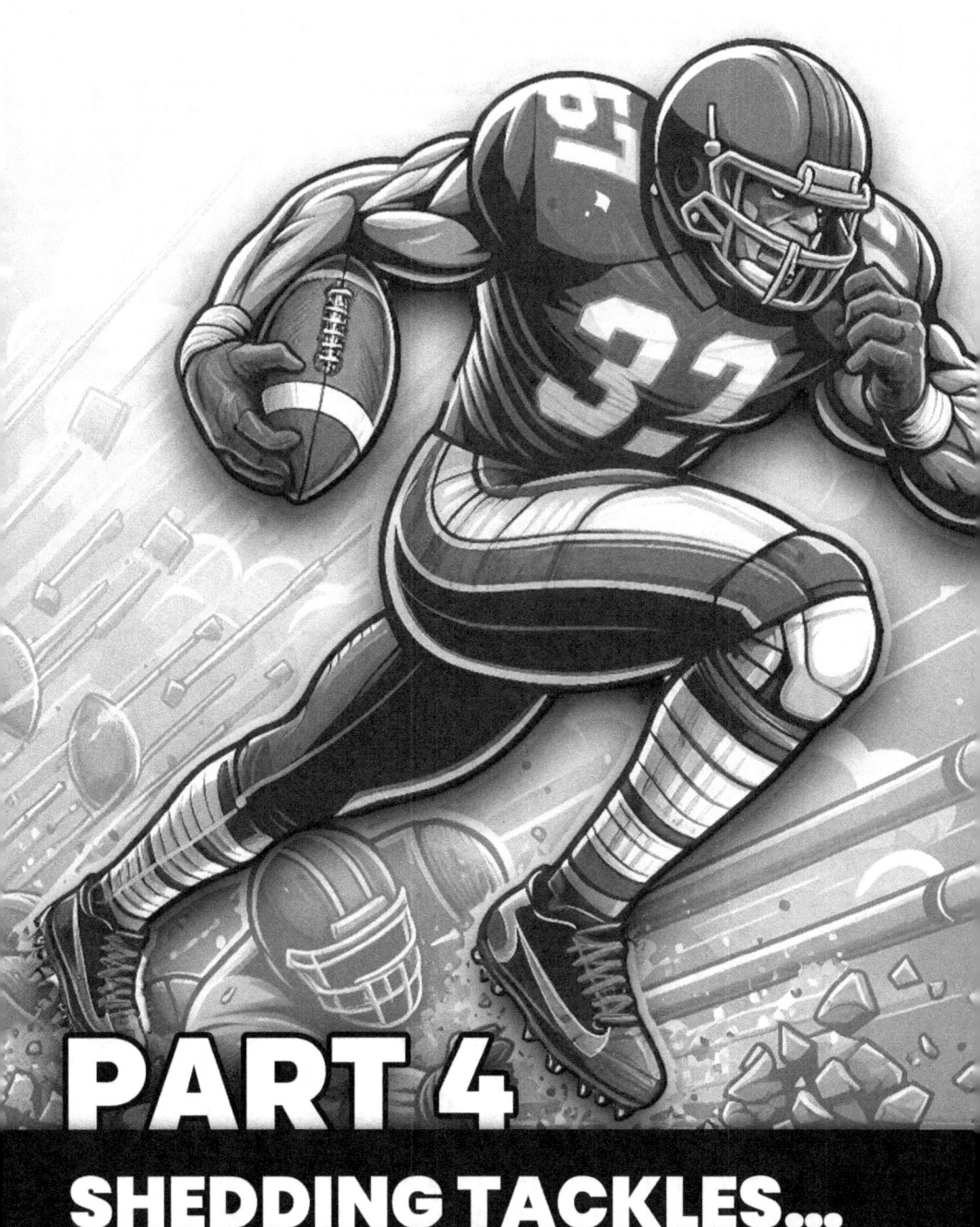

PART 4

SHEDDING TACKLES...
AND OBSTACLES

INDIANAPOLIS COLTS

WINNING IT FOR CHUCK

We all have dreams. Whether we're younger, or older, we all have something big that we want to accomplish in life. For Chuck Pagano, his dream was to be a successful NFL head coach. After all, he had spent the better part of his career as a college assistant coach, and an NFL positions coach. He wanted a shot at the big time.

In the 1980s and 1990s, Pagano worked his way up through the college coaching ranks. He coached everywhere, from USC, to the University of Miami, to Boise State, to East Carolina and UNLV. He even got his shot as a position coach in the NFL, working for the Browns, Raiders, and Ravens. Chuck even became the Ravens defensive coordinator in 2011. But he finally became a head coach at 49 years old, when Colts owner Jim Irsay hired Chuck to turn a struggling team around.

The Indianapolis Colts were especially bad. They were coming off a 2-14 season. Peyton Manning, their Hall of Fame quarterback, had missed the entire year in 2011 with a serious neck injury, and was released by the Colts afterward. Not only that, the Colts also were so bad they had the number one pick in the 2012 NFL Draft.

Coach Pagano was certainly going to have his work cut out for him while he tried to rebuild the team. But turning around a bad football team would be a cakewalk compared to another battle he would have to fight. In September 2012, right as he began his first season as head coach of the Indianapolis Colts, Chuck Pagano was diagnosed with leukemia (blood cancer). This was a devastating blow not only for Chuck and the Colts, but also for his family. His wife Tina, and three daughters Tara, Taylor, and Tori, had supported his passion for his career and the game of football wherever he coached. Now they would have to support him as he fought for his life.

Chuck had worked so hard to become an NFL head coach. Now it was all on the verge of being taken away from him in an instant. But surprisingly, he wasn't scared. He was just frustrated. "It's just like 'Why me? Why now?' You just get your dream job. The opportunity of a lifetime. You've got a wife and three daughters and three granddaughters counting on you. So it can't be true."

Sadly, it was true. Chuck would have to face his cancer battle head on. There was no turning back. But something he had heard from one of his veteran players, pass rusher Robert Mathis, inspired him to face his upcoming battle with true courage. "I remember Robert Mathis after the Jacksonville game. He said, 'There's no pity parties in life. There's no pity parties in football. We'll man up, come in tomorrow, watch the tape and we'll move on. We'll get better.' Those words kind of resonated with me. So I just looked at the doctor and said, 'What are my chances? What are the odds? What's the gameplan and what do I gotta do to beat this?'"

Chuck spent nearly a month in the hospital receiving chemotherapy, drugs and chemicals used to treat his cancer. Once he got out, he spent two more months at home going through the treatments that his doctors prescribed for him. But through all that, he watched his football team closely. Assistant coach Bruce Arians was leading the way for the Colts while Chuck was recovering. And quarterback Andrew Luck had a surprisingly good rookie season. He even led Indianapolis on several game-winning comeback drives!

Just like Coach Pagano, the Colts were slowly but surely fighting back. They weren't anybody's punching bag anymore. They weren't a laughingstock. In fact, they were a young, strong team legitimately fighting for a spot in the Playoffs as the season went on. And Chuck Pagano saw his team fight every week, whether he was in a hospital bed, or at home with his wife, daughters, and granddaughters. He loved his girls with all his heart, but he had to watch his team fight. And they were doing just that.

Years later, he was a guest on the Pat McAfee Show, a podcast and sports show hosted by one of his former players, punter Pat McAfee. And he told Pat that watching the Colts win during the 2012 season was the best cancer treatment he'd ever received. "Just watching you guys play, and watching Andrew and the fourth quarter comebacks. One after another, after another. That was the best medicine I could have ever received. They inspired me."

Chuck's courage inspired the Colts as well. The team rolled to a 10-5 record going into Week 17 of the regular season. Andrew Luck played so well that he made the Pro Bowl as a rookie. Not only that, nine of the team's 10 wins up to that point had been by a touchdown or less. It was meant to be. The Colts were on the verge of capping off a magical comeback season, and their once cancer-stricken coach was a new man. After spending three months on an exhausting chemotherapy treatment schedule, Chuck had done it. His cancer was in remission. It was gone. He had won the battle. He was free. And he was finally ready to return!

The Colts had a chance. And with Chuck Pagano back, they had all the emotional energy a team could need. They were jacked up, excited and ready to go. They had a chance to clinch a postseason berth with a win at home against the Houston Texans. Lucas Oil Stadium would be filled to capacity—63,000 Colts fans would be ready to roar for their team, for their shot at the playoffs, and for Chuck.

Just like most of the season, the Colts found themselves in a tight battle the entire day with Houston. They were in danger of losing just their second game decided by a touchdown or less. It was a back-and-forth seesaw battle all game long. But one big play would set off a party that had been brewing for weeks. After Houston had taken their one and only lead of the day, Colts return man Deji Karim responded by catching the football on a kickoff, finding a seam, running upfield, and then turning on the afterburner. He left the entire Texans special teams unit in the dust as he barreled toward paydirt. Karim took a kickoff 101 yards for the game-sealing touchdown. The Colts won 28-16!

The party was on in Indianapolis! Not only did the Colts win their 11th game of the season, they did it for Chuck Pagano. In the locker room after the game, Colts owner Jim Irsay handed Chuck Pagano the game ball. A visibly emotional Pagano reminded his team to live in the moment, and not let outside circumstances hold them back: "You refused to live in circumstances, and you decided consciously as a team and as a family, to live in a vision. That's why you're already champions and well on your way. I've got circumstances. You guys understand that. I understand it. It's already beat. My vision that I'm living, is to see two more daughters get married and dance at their weddings. I'm dancing at two more weddings, and we're hoisting that trophy together!"

Beyond the 2012 season, Chuck Pagano coached the Colts until 2017. Unfortunately, he never won a Lombardi Trophy and Super Bowl Championship like he hoped he would. But he did something far greater than winning a World Championship.

He showed every single one of his 53 players, every Colts fan, and the entire world, to never give up in spite of the circumstances that life throws their way. He's already a champion for winning his fight against cancer, even if he doesn't have a Super Bowl ring.

Chuck's courage can be a great lesson for you as you go through life. You should always chase after your dreams and goals. But life will force you to take paths you don't expect. And how you respond to them will determine how the rest of your journey goes. A lot of people wallow in self-pity. They feel sorry for themselves when life beats them down. But people who are champions both on and off the field don't let their circumstances define who they are. They fight through them. Chuck Pagano fought against cancer with courage and won. And now he's enjoying his best life with his wife, daughters, and granddaughters.

Whenever life throws negative circumstances your way, remember how Chuck Pagano handled his. Simply get up, dust yourself off, move forward, and keep going each day. There is no hurdle or circumstance in life that you can't overcome. Chuck Pagano is living proof of that!

· His younger brother John Pagano is a coach with the Washington Commanders.

· Chuck Pagano is a devout Christian and credits his faith in Jesus with helping him beat leukemia.

· Chuck hosted a program on ESPN during the 2022 NFL season called "Coach P's Keys" where he analyzed the games each week. He's still in the studio from time to time as an expert analyst.

· Was head coach of the Indianapolis Colts from 2012-2017.

· Named Coach of the Year in 2012.

· Earned the George S. Halas Award in 2013 for overcoming his battle with leukemia.

· Was a college and NFL assistant coach for almost 20 years before finally getting his shot as a head coach with the Colts.

· Has a wife and three daughters.

· Played college football at Wyoming from 1981-1984 as a safety.

· He's a frequent guest on The Pat McAfee Show, a podcast hosted by one of his former players, Pat McAfee.

1. Before becoming head coach of the Colts, what position group did Chuck Pagano coach?

2. True or False: Chuck Pagano served as the defensive coordinator for the Bears after leaving the Colts.

3. While Chuck Pagano coached the Colts, which wide receiver broke the single season record for receiving yards by a rookie?

4. Who was the coach of the Colts while Chuck Pagano was recovering from leukemia?

5. What was the Colts' best record under Coach Pagano?

6. Who did the Colts eventually lose to in the 2012 Playoffs?

7. True or False: The Colts had only three Pro Bowlers in 2012.

8. True or False: Andrew Luck won Rookie of the Year in 2012 with the Colts.

9. True or False: Butch Davis gave Chuck Pagano his first NFL coaching job.

10. True or False: Chuck Pagano retired at the end of the 2021 season.

ANSWER

1. He was a defensive backs coach for several teams.
2. True.
3. T.Y. Hilton.
4. Bruce Arians.
5. 11-5.
6. They lost to the eventual Super Bowl Champion Baltimore Ravens.
7. True! Robert Mathis, Reggie Wayne and Andrew Luck made it to the Pro Bowl that year.
8. False. Although Luck had an outstanding rookie season, Robert Griffin III won that award with the Washington Redskins.
9. True! Chuck followed Butch to Cleveland, where he was the Browns' secondary coach under him from 2001-2004.
10. True.

QUOTES FROM CHUCK PAGANO

"We have to know that nothing is promised. Nothing is guaranteed. Especially tomorrow."

"If you don't have your health, you don't have anything."

"I am the luckiest man in the world."

"You are defined by how you play the game. Not by the game itself."

"When you have things taken away, you promise you'll never take anything for granted ever again."

LESSONS FROM STORY

· Life can change in a blink. So enjoy every moment and live it to the fullest.

· Lean on family and friends during weak times. Chuck Pagano leaned on his family and friends.

· Seeing others succeed even when you're struggling can really fire you up!

· It's important to have goals and visions for yourself.

· Support your friends and family members in their passions and careers, even during the toughest times.

LARRY BROWN
SILENT TRIUMPH

Even for the best prospects, it's an uphill climb to make it into the National Football League. And that's just to make it onto a team's roster for the regular season. The percentage of players who truly make their mark on the league is even smaller. But Larry Brown, a running back who played for the Washington Redskins from 1967 to 1976, didn't just make it to the league—he left a legacy that can still be felt today.

Brown was drafted in the 8th round of the 1969 NFL Draft, #191 overall out of Kansas State. He wasn't supposed to be a star player—he wasn't even close to it in terms of talent. He had primarily been a blocking running back during his college career with the Kansas State Wildcats. He didn't get to run the football very much. He was an afterthought. Even though Larry Brown wasn't the last player taken in the 1969 NFL Draft, he probably felt like he was. In today's NFL language, the player who is taken last in the Draft every year is called "Mr. Irrelevant."

At the start of Larry Brown's NFL journey, he was low in the Draft, wasn't seen as a threat to run the football, and he was in an offense that had three of the top five wide receivers in the league. The Redskins were a pass-first football team when Brown arrived in Washington, DC. But as luck would have it, the Redskins, coached by NFL legend Vince Lombardi in 1969, needed a productive running back to take the pressure off quarterback Sonny Jurgensen. Jurgensen was a decorated but aging gunslinger who was near the end of his career.

Lombardi saw something special in Larry Brown when Brown first arrived as a rookie in 1969. He loved the young running back's willingness to run with power and authority. Brown was only 5'11 and 195 pounds. But he ran like a man who was 6'3 and 230 pounds. He was a punishing running back, and not afraid to dish out vicious hits to anyone who tried to tackle him! But for as talented as Larry Brown was, Lombardi noticed something peculiar. When Jurgensen snapped the football during games, Brown was slightly late getting out of his stance and into his block or running route. Lombardi later found out the cause of the problem: Brown was completely deaf in one ear.

Instead of listening for the quarterback's snap count to know when to move, Larry would watch for when his offensive linemen would move, and then either spring into his block or explode forward to run with the football. But in a game where defensive players are fast enough to react in a split second, that wasn't fast enough. So Vince Lombardi came up with a clever idea—to have an earpiece installed in Brown's helmet. He lobbied and petitioned NFL Commissioner Pete Rozelle for the earpiece, and after approval from the league, Brown was allowed to use an earpiece during games to better hear the snap count. Once Brown was allowed to do that, he took care of the football and became one of the most explosive running backs in the league!

In his rookie season in 1969, Brown ran for 888 yards and four touchdowns while giving Washington a reliable running back who averaged 4.4 yards per carry. He was one of the big reasons why the Redskins went 7-5-2 that year, which was their first winning season since 1955. Brown was also selected to his first Pro Bowl, the NFL's version of an All-Star game that featured the league's best players.

Brown went to four straight Pro Bowls from 1969 to 1972. Fans appreciated his tough running style, which he developed after surviving in Pittsburgh's Hill District, a tough neighborhood. But Larry wasn't just a great running back. He got a shot at ultimate glory against the ultimate team. Brown, quarterback Billy Kilmer, and a defense nicknamed the "Over the Hill Gang" even appeared in Super Bowl 7. In that game, they were matched up against Don Shula's Miami Dolphins, who had gone a perfect 14-0 during the regular season. While Larry Brown had an MVP season in 1972, rushing for over 1,200 yards and eight touchdowns, a stout Miami defense unfortunately never let him get going that day. The Dolphins held Brown to just 72 yards on 22 carries, and ended up winning the Super Bowl, 14-7.

After one more solid season in 1973 where he ran for 860 yards and eight touchdowns, Brown's production began to decline dramatically due to several injuries. He was the hard-nosed runner that a lot of football fans love to watch. But in an era where many of the NFL's best running backs were well over 200 pounds, the tough running took its toll on his body, and he eventually retired in 1976 at just 29 years old.

Larry Brown's career was probably shorter than he would have wanted. But that's the nature of playing as a running back in the National Football League. Many running backs are extremely talented, but they often have short careers since they put their body through a lot of punishment every Sunday. But Larry Brown was unlike any other running back in NFL history. He may not be considered the greatest running back to ever play, and his career did not last as long as some other running backs, but Brown was different and special—he was one of only four memorable deaf players who made their mark on the league.

He had just as much of a desire to succeed as the league's greatest legends. All he needed was the work ethic to make it happen, and a helping hand from a caring coach who saw something truly special in him. Larry Brown had both of those things. He grew up as a tough Pittsburgh kid who had to earn everything he worked for in his life. And even though Vince Lombardi was in his final season as an NFL coach when Brown was a rookie, he never lost his desire to help his players become the best versions of themselves. Larry Brown was perhaps the last great player that Lombardi ever coached before he passed away from cancer in 1970.

Brown's legacy is complete. Over the course of his career, he made the Pro Bowl four straight times, was in the Top 5 for rushing yards three times, led the league in rushing yards in 1970, and was the first Washington running back to gain more than 1,000 yards in a single season. To top it all off, Larry Brown is in both the Washington Commanders Ring of Fame, and the Washington, DC, Sports Hall of Fame.

Larry Brown never came close to making it to the Pro Football Hall of Fame. But sometimes, the love of a city and its fans can be an even bigger and lasting reward than receiving a bronze bust and gold jacket in Canton, Ohio. Larry Brown is still beloved in Washington, DC, even if his playing days are long over. Even though he retired from football in 1976, Larry Brown remains active in the Washington, DC, area to this day in his late seventies. He can frequently be seen at Commanders games, and helps out with the Prince George's County Special Olympics.

For every kid out there who has a unique obstacle in life, take a cue from Larry Brown—no obstacle is ever too big to overcome. Whether you are deaf, blind, or disabled in any way, you have a purpose. Focus on your dream and go for it! It might take you a little longer to get there. Or you might need a helping hand from someone, like Larry Brown needed help from Vince Lombardi. But everyone has a purpose, even if it may not seem like it at times.

And once you fully use your talents and gifts to grab that purpose, you won't only enjoy your purpose, you'll also inspire others as well. People will see how hard you work, and it will influence them to do the same. No hurdle is too high to climb. No challenge is unbeatable. Whenever you think you won't reach your goals, just remember Larry Brown. He never gave up, Neither should you!

· He was born on September 19, 1947 in Clairton, Pennsylvania.

· He appeared in four Pro Bowls and a Super Bowl with the Redskins.

· He required a hearing aid to be able to do his job as a running back. He was deaf in one ear.

· Named as one of the 70 Greatest Washington Redskins of All Time.

· Larry Brown grew up playing baseball instead of football. His dad, a former baseball player, wanted his son to follow in his footsteps.

· Even though he was a running back in the NFL, Larry played fullback in high school. He wasn't afraid to hit people. He believed that being physical helped him make a statement.

· He initially wanted to be a baseball star before changing his mind.

· Legendary head coach Vince Lombardi was Larry Brown's head coach his rookie season.

· He was named NFL MVP in 1972.

· He was taken in the 8th round of the 1969 NFL Draft.

1. Which team did Larry Brown and the Redskins play against in the Super Bowl in 1972?

2. True or False: Larry Brown was the first running back to rush for 1,000 yards in Washington football history.

3. Where did Larry Brown play college football?

4. Before Larry Brown was drafted by the Redskins in 1969, how many losing seasons did the team have in a row?

5. True or False: Larry Brown had 50 rushing touchdowns in his career.

6. Was Larry Brown's yards per carry average above or below four yards per carry?

7. True or False: Larry Brown is in the Hall of Fame.

8. True or False: Larry Brown had more than 5,000 rushing yards in his career.

9. True or False: Larry Brown is rarely seen in public anymore.

10. What made Larry Brown a tough running back in his own words?

ANSWER

1. The legendary 1972 Miami Dolphins.
2. True!
3. Kansas State
4. 13.
5. False. He had 35 rushing touchdowns.
6. Below. 3.8 yards per carry.
7. False.
8. True. He had 5,875 rushing yards.
9. False. Larry Brown is often out and about, and involved with many charitable causes in the Washington DC area.
10. Growing up in a tough neighborhood in Pittsburgh.

QUOTES FROM LARRY BROWN

"I've grown up playing for some incredible coaches, and I don't think anybody's ever been as fortunate as I have in terms of the people I've been allowed to play under, coach under, or be involved with."

"The first five were my favorite years. At the time it was just Jim Brown, O.J. Simpson and me. I thought that was pretty good company."

"How good a back was he? Well, when you talk about running backs, you only talk four people - Jim Brown, Gale Sayers, O.J. Larry Brown. A lot of backs had the ability to do what Larry did, but very few of them had the desire." -Charley Taylor

"The greatest game I ever saw Larry play was in New York in 1972. They tore his hands up, he was bleeding everywhere, people were throwing stuff at him from the stands. But he still gained 191 yards that day. The man was just determined. You could see it in his eyes. He always had that look when he played. When we were down, he'd always fire us up. He was that kind of guy, and he's going to be missed." -Charley Taylor

LESSONS FROM STORY

· Sometimes all you need is a helping hand to achieve greatness.

· Coaches and mentors who care about you can make all the difference.

· People with disabilities can be just as successful as physically able bodied people.

· You'll be loved for your effort far more than you will be for your talent.

· If you work hard enough, a lot of doors can open up for you.

SHAQUEM GRIFFIN

SILENCING THE DOUBTERS

Every NFL player's journey to the league is unique. Some are seen by scouts as undersized, like Drew Brees and Baker Mayfield. Others are called "unathletic," like Bernie Kosar. But very few NFL players have a story that is as unique as Shaquem Griffin. Why is he so unique? Well, he played in the NFL for four seasons with only one hand.

When Shaquem Griffin was born on July 20, 1995, to Terry and Tangie Griffin, doctors initially thought he'd arrived into the world as a healthy baby along with his twin brother Shaquill. But then doctors soon noticed something was wrong with Shaquem: the fingers on his left hand weren't formed properly. Shaquem was born with something called Constriction Ring Syndrome or CRS. This is an extremely rare condition that affects roughly only five out of 10,000 people at birth. In Shaquem's case, the umbilical cord became so tightly wrapped around his left hand, that it not only prevented the hand from forming properly, it also cut off circulation.

Once Shaquem was born and freed from the umbilical cord, he reached his growth milestones like any normal baby should, even if his left hand didn't form properly. Shaquem had managed to live with his condition without any major issues, although he was always dealing with some level of pain, but one night, the pain became too much for him to handle. It got so bad that he walked out to the kitchen and grabbed a knife. He was about to cut his hand off until his mother stopped him and took the knife from him. An emergency surgery was scheduled for him the next day.

Shaquem had his entire hand removed. There was only a stump left where his left hand used to be. But while most kids his age would've been extremely upset growing up without a hand, the surgery actually had the exact opposite effect on Shaquem. It freed him from his pain, and still allowed him to play sports and be an active boy. Shaquem was still an energetic, passionate boy. He would just have to figure out different, creative ways to still do the things he loved to do. But he was determined to make it work. His parents never discouraged his dreams either. If anything, they pushed Shaquem harder.

Shaquem's father, Terry, always tried to help Shaquem find ways to do things on his own as he grew up, whether that was weightlifting, doing pushups, sit-ups, dips, and other exercises. It was always important to both of Shaquem's parents that they help him continue to be independent despite having only one hand. "Everything he wanted it to do, it was like 'Well, we're going to test it out so we can find a way you can do it on your own. I test it out with one hand. If I can do it with one hand, you can do it with one hand.'"

This approach showed Shaquem he could still do anything he put his mind to. And it not only strengthened him physically, it also helped build his character and toughened him up as well. "The attitude towards me was never allowing me to make excuses. Treat me like everybody else. If you're hard on my brother, you're hard on me."

With this mindset in place, Shaquem began to pursue his football dreams. His twin brother Shaquill did the same. While Shaquill received a bunch of scholarship offers from big-time colleges as a cornerback, Shaquem did not have the same success as a linebacker. At this point, it would probably be easy for a case of sibling rivalry to develop. Especially when one is seen as more successful than the other. But that wasn't the case for the Griffin brothers. Shaquem enjoyed the success that Shaquill was having, and Shaquill never looked down on his brother.

But here's where their story takes a heartwarming turn: Shaquill received offers to play as a cornerback at Florida, Florida State, Miami, and several other schools. And he had the talent to be a star for the Gators, Seminoles, or Hurricanes. But Shaquill turned them all down. Why? He wasn't going to play for a school unless Shaquem was recruited as well. He wasn't playing football without his brother. The two had dreams of accomplishing all their big life goals together. This was just another one on the list. "We were going to live together, play together, we were going to marry twins, we were going to have twin kids," Shaquill said. "It was about sticking with my brother. And that bond and love I have for him is way bigger than some scholarship."

Central Florida's coach at the time, George O'Leary, understood the brotherly bond that the two had. The UCF Knights were the only ones who were willing to take both Griffin brothers on scholarship, and they did exactly that! Shaquem wasn't quite as talented as his brother. But he was happy for Shaquill. He rode the bench as he saw his brother excel as a cornerback. That is until new coach Scott Frost gave him a chance to play in 2016.

Under Frost's watch, Shaquem finally excelled. That year, he was in the Top 15 in the country in sacks as UCF's best and most fearsome pass rusher. In 2017, he was even better and near his peak as a college football player. He was the unquestioned leader of UCF's defense, was one of the captains for the Knights, and was named the American Athletic Conference Defensive Player of the year. Not only that, he led UCF to their first ever 13-0 season, and a final ranking of #6 in the Top 25 poll!

He was now all set to take the NFL by storm, right? No, not exactly. Even though he had played some of the best football of his life, NFL scouts still doubted whether Shaquem could play as a linebacker at the highest level. But their prejudice against him for having just one hand only added fuel to his fire. And before the 2018 NFL Draft, Shaquem did something that no other linebacker in NFL history has done before or since—he ran a blazing fast 40-yard dash. He ran the dash in just 4.38 seconds. That was the fastest 40-yard dash time recorded for any NFL linebacker. Ever. He made most of the scouts look stupid for doubting him. But the team that was smart enough to take him, the Seattle Seahawks, grabbed Shaquem with the 141st overall pick in the fifth round of the Draft. He'd made it. And not only that, he was also reunited with his brother Shaquill. It was a dream come true!

Shaquem played in the NFL for four seasons, and was mostly a contributor on special teams covering kickoffs and punts. He unfortunately didn't fully realize his dream of being a star linebacker in the league. But for a man with one hand, he still was one of the very few players who were good enough to be chosen by an NFL team to play for them. He still suited up and played his absolute best from 2018 to 2021 before retiring from the sport. That's more than most of us get to do in a lifetime.

Even though he's now retired, Shaquem still stays close to the sport he loves. He's now a part of the NFL Legends Community, which is a community of former NFL players who serve as mentors to other former players, and current players who need help or life advice. He pays it forward. And his journey came from a simple mindset—that is, showing people that he could do anything. "I wanted to show everybody that if there's something somebody says that you can't do, the only person stopping you is yourself."

While this story has an inspiring message for everyone, I especially encourage kids who have conditions and disabilities to read this story as often as possible. It does not matter if you're blind, deaf, missing a limb, have cerebral palsy, or anything else. You can do anything that you put your mind to. Don't let anyone tell you that you can't do something.

Shaquem Griffin didn't allow his life situation, or other people to drag him down. He continues to inspire millions around the world to chase after their dreams no matter what situation they are in. If you have the same mindset, you will also inspire others!

• Shaquem Griffin was born on July 20, 1995.

• He's only 60 seconds younger than his twin brother.

• In addition to being a football player growing up, Shaquem was also a track and field athlete. He competed in the 4x100 relay, triple jump, shot put and discus.

• When he won the triple jump state title in Florida, LSU, Miami and Purdue tried to recruit him.

• Shaquem received the 2019 NCAA Inspiration Award, which is awarded to current or former NCAA athletes who show exceptional courage when dealing with life-altering situations.

• His brother is named Shaquill.

• Shaquill was not going to play at any college unless they accepted Shaquem. That's how close they are. They both played for the University of Central Florida (UCF) Knights football team.

• They both briefly played together for the Seattle Seahawks.

• He once slept at the UCF football facility. That's how much he loves the game.

• He once did 20 bench presses of 225 pounds during the NFL Combine while wearing a prosthetic hand.

1. What condition was Shaquem Griffin born with?

2. True or false: Shaquem Griffin only played for the Seahawks during his NFL career.

3. True or False: Shaquem wrote a book with his brother Shaquill.

4. True or False: Shaquem Griffin often slept in his football jersey the night before a game when he was a kid.

5. True or False: Shaquem Griffin became the first player with one hand to start an NFL game.

6. True or False: Shaquem Griffin's 40-yard time was the fastest for any linebacker since 2003.

7. Shaquem Griffin already has his own ESPN 30 for 30.

8. How many tackles did Shaquem Griffin Record in his first NFL game?

9. What famous college football award was Shaquem Griffin nominated for during his time playing football at UCF?

10. What number did Shaquem Griffin wear during his football career?

ANSWER

1. *He was born with an extremely rare condition called amniotic band syndrome.*
2. *False. He was also a member of the Miami Dolphins.*
3. *True. The Griffin brothers wrote a book called Inseparable: How Family and Sacrifice Forged a Path to the NFL..*
4. *True.*
5. *True.*
6. *True.*
7. *False. But he does have his own documentary called Shaquem Griffin: Will Finds a Way.*
8. *Shaquem registered six tackles during his first NFL game with the Seahawks.*
9. *He was nominated for the Chuck Bednarik Award, which is given to the best defensive player in college football, but did not win.*
10. *49.*

"No matter if you have one hand or two hands, when someone tells you that you can't do something, the only thing you can do is just prove them wrong, no matter what it is, no matter how hard it is."

"Nobody was ever going to tell me that I didn't belong on a football field. And nobody was ever going to tell me that I couldn't be great."

"I'm gonna be called Shaquem Griffin the football player, not Shaquem Griffin the one-hand wonder."

"I'm always going to be smiling. I'm always going to be in a good mood."

"You're not disabled unless you say 'I'm disabled.'"

LESSONS FROM STORY

· If your parents or role models in your life push you, it means they care about you, and they want to see you do your best.

· Even if you have a condition, you can still do things. You just might need to figure out a creative way to do them.

· Family is everything, and sibling bonds are the best!

· Even if you aren't the most athletic, hard work can cover a lot of weaknesses.

· Even if no one else is there for you, true family, whether they're biologically related to you or not, will always be there for you.

TOM DEMPSEY

THE GOLDEN FOOT

The NFL has existed for over 100 years. Over the course of a century, the league has seen several different players make their mark. Each has their own unique journey and story to tell. But nobody has a more unique story than kicker Tom Dempsey.

Dempsey played for five different teams over the course of his 10-year career as a placekicker. He kicked for the Saints, Eagles, Rams, Oilers, and Bills. But what makes him so unique and special is that he was born without any toes on his right foot, or any fingers on his right hand. But he didn't let his condition affect him. He played high school football in Southern California after moving out there from Milwaukee, Wisconsin. But while he was playing high school football, he played under a coach who taught him about discipline and mental toughness.

Dempsey's high school football coach was a former

United States Marine who taught all his players, Dempsey included, to improvise, adapt and overcome no matter what their situation was. He encouraged Dempsey but never gave him special treatment because of his condition. Dempsey was also sparked toward great things in the NFL by something his coach did during his senior year at San Dieguito High School. Near the end of that final home game in 1965, every senior was pulled out of the game while the crowd cheered. Every senior was pulled out except for one. Dempsey stayed in for the rest of the game.

After the game, Dempsey walked off the field, confused. "Coach, why did you leave me in the game?"

His coach looked at him without batting an eye and said, "Tom, after this game, most of your teammates are done playing. But you're going places." Tom's coach was right. He ended up playing college football at Palomar College before making it into the NFL as a free agent.

He went undrafted in 1968, but that didn't matter to Tom. He was getting a chance to play the game he loved. He initially signed with the Chargers practice squad before being signed by the New Orleans Saints in 1969. He made 22 out of 41 field goals during his first full season in the league. That might not sound very impressive at first. Especially when the best kickers in today's game are nearly automatic. They rarely miss. But kickers who played back in Tom Dempsey's day didn't kick like they do today. When Dempsey played, kickers usually kicked straight on, or with the top of their kicking foot. Kickers in today's NFL usually kick like soccer players, or with the side of their foot.

Not only did Dempsey kick off the top of his foot despite not having any toes, but he also had to kick with a specially made shoe. It basically looked like a box for his foot since he didn't have any toes. Even with this disadvantage, he still managed to make 22 field goals during his rookie season, including seven out of 11 field goals from 40-49 yards, and one from 55 yards. He did so well that he earned his first and only Pro Bowl selection after that year!

However, what Tom Dempsey is most known for occurred during his second season in the NFL on November 8, 1970. The Saints were having an awful season that year. They'd only won two out of 14 games. The Detroit Lions came down to New Orleans, and were playing the Saints extremely tough. Both teams played a tough, hard-fought back and forth game. But near the end of it, Detroit led New Orleans 17-16 with just two seconds left. The game was all but over. The only way that New Orleans had a chance to win was from a 63-yard field goal.

No kicker in the history of the National Football League had ever made a kick from that distance at that time. And no one playing for the Saints or the Lions that day thought it would happen either. Dempsey's New Orleans teammate Dan Abramowicz said exactly what everyone was thinking at the time just before Dempsey was sent out to attempt the kick: "I thought we had lost our mind. I was walking down the sidelines towards the tunnel in Tulane Stadium to go into the locker room. I thought we had lost our mind."

One of Detroit's players was eager to stick around and watch Dempsey miss the kick. Lions linebacker Wayne Walker thought there was little to no chance that Detroit would lose the game. "I was on my way into the locker room, basically. I just thought I'd stop and watch him miss it and go on in with the win."

Saints safety Joe Scarpati was going to be the holder for Dempsey's kick. He knew it was going to be a long kick, but wasn't sure how long. Years after the game, he says that he's grateful he didn't know how long the kick was. "We knew it was far. But we didn't know it was 63. We know if somebody would've said, 'hey this is a 63-yard field goal,' we probably would've tightened up. But we just kind of did it out of reaction rather than thinking."

While many of his Saints teammates were nervous, Tom Dempsey wasn't. He treated the 63-yard attempt that was in front of him just like any other kick he'd made during his career. "I was basically thinking about the same things that I did every time I kicked. 'Keep your head down, kick through the ball, but kick this one a little bit harder than you normally do.'"

And with that, Dempsey took two steps forward, and booted the ball as hard as he could with his right leg as it sailed through the air at old Tulane Stadium. As the ball traveled end over end, it just seemed to keep going forever. As the ball was in the air, Saints quarterback Billy Kilmer had no doubt that his teammate and friend had just hit a game-winner. The longest game-winner in NFL history at the time. "The moment he hit the ball, I said, 'My god, he made it.' You could just see that ball fire off his foot."

The ball traveled through the air...and went through the uprights with less than a yard to spare. Dempsey did it! A kicker born with no toes on his right foot had just made the longest field goal in NFL history! Years later, Dempsey was happy that people still recognized him for hitting that game-winning field goal. But he also recognized that there were more important things that had happened in his life than making that field goal. "I don't really think it was larger than life," he said. "There's been a lot of other things in my life that I consider more important than the field goal. I think probably the most important thing to me is my family. My boy, my two little girls and my wife. I think the biggest thrill I've ever had is the day they were born."

Years later, Dempsey's record was surpassed by Matt Prater when he kicked a 64-yard field goal for the Denver Broncos against the Tennessee Titans. Justin Tucker of the Baltimore Ravens currently holds the NFL record for the longest field goal, when he booted a 66-yarder to defeat the Detroit Lions as time ran out in 2021. But Dempsey's field goal is still impressive. It's the third-longest field goal in NFL history. And the lessons he taught everybody by making that field goal will live on forever.

Tom Dempsey passed away in 2020 at the age of 73. But he is immortalized in Saints and football history. A man born in Milwaukee, Wisconsin, showed what was possible if you only had belief in yourself, plenty of practice, and a chance to succeed. What he did can be a lesson to everyone, but especially to those of you who have a disability. If you do have a disability, no matter what it is, you still can accomplish your goals. A lot of people may tell you that you can't. Don't listen to them.

You might have to do certain things a little differently to achieve your goals and succeed in life and that's okay. But the main thing to do is never give up. Try, try, and try again if needed, but never give up. Tom Dempsey could have given up when things got hard for him. But he didn't. He powered through his adversity, never made excuses, and never felt sorry for himself. And now he's part of one of the greatest moments in NFL history.

If you follow Tom Dempsey's example, you too can one day inspire others. Whether that's on the football field or off, you have a chance to help elevate others and make them believe in their own dreams!

· Played as a lineman in high school before switching over to kicker.

· Wasn't just born without the toes on his right foot, he was missing the fingers on his right hand as well.

· His 63-yard field goal to beat the Detroit Lions was an NFL record at one time.

· Born on January 12, 1947 in Milwaukee, Wisconsin, but soon moved to Southern California with his family.

· Used to do one-handed chin-ups to impress his classmates in grade school.

· Was a star baseball player for his high school. He also did track and field and wrestling in addition to doing football.

· Tom's high school wrestling background enabled him to have good technique as a lineman. He probably could have been a decent NFL lineman if he hadn't been a kicker!

· Dempsey took up kicking as a "joke" while he was taking a break from regular practice in college.

· Dempsey was affectionately nicknamed "Stumpy" by his coaches and teammates.

· Before Dempsey's game-winning 63-yard kick against the Lions, the previous record had been from 56 yards. He shattered it!

1. Tom's condition has a scientific name. What is it?

2. What did Tom do after retiring from football?

3. Which Hall of Fame was he inducted into for his 63-yard field goal, and other accomplishments?

4. While Tom was nicknamed "Stumpy" by his coaches and teammates. He had another nickname. What was it?

5. How many teams did Tom Dempsey play for?

6. How many years did Tom Dempsey's record last for the longest field goal?

7. Who broke his record?

8. What tool was Dempsey's foot shaped like?

9. True or false: Some thought Dempsey's uniquely shaped shoe gave him an unfair advantage.

10. True or false: The NFL eventually made a rule nicknamed the "Tom Dempsey Rule."

ANSWER

1. Phocomelia.
2. He embarked on a career as a motivational speaker and assistant football coach.
3. The Louisiana Sports Hall of Fame.
4. The Toeless Wonder.
5. Five teams (Saints, Bills, Oilers, Eagles, Rams).
6. 43 years.
7. Matt Prater of the Denver Broncos made a 64-yard field goal in 2013.
8. Sledgehammer.
9. True. Cowboys owner Tex Schramm complained to the league.
10. True. The league eventually made a rule saying that all kickers, even ones with prosthetic or missing limbs, had to all wear the same type of shoe.

"You have to ignore all the external factors. Focus solely on that spot on the ground."

"Physical toughness is not tough. That's easy."

"I wouldn't trade that era of football for anything in the world. The guys you played with, and the guys you played against were very special."

"I've been a very fortunate man that I've always had great coaches. They always helped me and it was a lot of fun."

"Never read the newspaper. You're never as good as they make you out to be, and you're never as bad as they make you out to be."

LESSONS FROM STORY

· Don't use a disability as an excuse.

· You can find different ways to do something if you can't do it the normal way.

· There will always be people who don't like you. You can't listen to them. Just do your thing.

· Practice makes perfect.

· Use whatever God gave you, whether you're disabled or not.

ADRIAN PETERSON

COMFORT IN FOOTBALL

Adrian Peterson is now known as one of the most electrifying running backs in NFL history. But behind his highlight reel plays, and incredible speed and power, there is a side to him that most people do not know. They only see the incredible athlete, and cannot see the human being who wore the shoulder pads and jersey. But Adrian Peterson's story is a very human story.

Growing up as a kid in Palestine, Texas, Peterson was the son of two great athletes. Nelson Peterson was a star basketball player in college for Idaho State, while Adrian's mother Bonita Brown, was a Texas track and field star. But even though Adrian loved his parents growing up like any son would, the person he was closest to was his brother Brian.

Adrian idolized Brian, even though Brian was just two

years older than him. The two brothers were inseparable during their early years. Brian and Adrian Peterson did everything together. Their favorite thing to do though, was to footrace each other around their Palestine, Texas neighborhood. Both Peterson boys were incredibly fast. But according to Adrian, Brian was so much quicker. In fact, there were times that Brian would give Adrian a 20-yard head start during a race around the block, and Brian would still beat him! "We were extremely fast for kids. We were seven or eight, and we'd beat 15-and 16-year-old kids running. He used to burn off on me. He had so much potential."

Tragically, the potential that Brian Peterson had as an athlete would never be fully realized. While Brian and Adrian were playing one day, Brian was struck and killed by a drunk driver who was speeding through the neighborhood. He was only nine years old. This event would change Adrian's life forever. He would never get over the loss of his brother. But he knew that it would shape him into the man and athlete that he would soon become.

Adrian Peterson soon found comfort in the sport of football as he was growing up. And not only did he find comfort in it, but he also discovered that he was very, very good at it. In fact, when one of Peterson's youth coaches once saw him play, he swore that Peterson would one day make it to the NFL. The coach was right. Peterson had a dazzling career at the University of Oklahoma as a running back. In three years of playing for the Sooners from 2004 to 2006, Adrian Peterson had over 4,000 yards and 41 rushing touchdowns. He finished second in the Heisman voting in 2004, and was the first Oklahoma freshman to be recognized as a first-team All-American.

By the time Peterson was done with his Junior season at Oklahoma, he knew that he was ready to take a shot at the next level. So, he gave up his senior year of eligibility, and decided to enter the 2007 NFL Draft. But shortly before the Draft, tragedy struck him again. Adrian lost his half-brother, Chris. It put immense stress and pressure on Adrian to keep his emotions in check. But not only that, he still had to go out and perform well for the NFL scouts that had come to see him and other players at the NFL Combine.

The NFL Combine is a skills test for every player who is trying to get into the league. It measures all sorts of things, from strength, to speed, to the ability to understand plays and strategy. Adrian not only had to excel at all these things, but he had to do it while mourning his half-brother, who had passed away just the night before. But like he had done after his brother Brian had passed away all those years before, Adrian would again use football to help himself cope with the loss. He would throw himself into the sport with everything he had, and show every scout there, that their team would be wise to draft him. The Minnesota Vikings were smart when they took him 7th overall. It would be one of the best decisions that the team would ever make.

As soon as he put on that purple and gold jersey for the first time, Peterson immediately began to set ambitious goals for himself, like being named the Offensive Rookie of the Year. He would eventually win that award after racking up 1,341 yards and 12 rushing touchdowns. He was so fast and explosive that many were comparing him to Hall of Fame running back Eric Dickerson. Most running backs are either fast, or powerful. But rarely are they both at the same time. Running backs who have speed and explosiveness are a rare breed in any level of football. Adrian Peterson is a prime example of that kind of running back.

Through the first nine seasons of his career from 2007 to 2015, Peterson was arguably the best running back in all of football. He routinely rushed for over 1,200 yards and double-digit touchdowns each season. But his crowning achievement as a pro football player came in the 2012 season, when he rushed for over 2,000 yards and 12 touchdowns. Not only was he the league's leading rusher, he was also named the NFL's

Most Valuable Player at 27 years old. That year, he was on top of the football world.

However, just as he was going to take things to even greater heights, everything came crashing down in 2013. That year, Adrian learned he had a two-year old son that he hadn't known about. He was overjoyed and planned to meet the little boy, but never got the chance. Weeks after Peterson learned that he was the boy's father, the boy passed away. Up to this point, Adrian Peterson had mainly used football to help handle the tragedies in his life. But this was one tragedy too many. And so he leaned on his faith to help cope with his latest loss. Peterson decided to play just two days later. He only ran for 62 yards in a blowout loss for the Vikings. But just being out there after a third big tragedy in his life, took enormous emotional strength. But he played on.

Through the last three seasons of his career, Peterson struggled with injuries. But that was only because he had played so hard while he was in his prime. The shelf life of a typical running back in the NFL is 8–10 years. They don't last very long in the league. But Adrian Peterson was anything but a typical running back. After everything was said and done, he rushed for almost 15,000 yards, which put him 5th on the all-time rushing list. He also scored 120 rushing touchdowns over 15 years.

On the surface, Adrian Peterson's story looks like one of nothing but tragedy. But that couldn't be further from the truth. It's also a story of great triumph and overcoming the trials of life. Like an earlier story in this book about Chuck Pagano and the 2012 Indianapolis Colts, Adrian Peterson made the most of his time in football in spite of his circumstances, just like Coach Pagano did. And because he continued to fight through tragedy, Adrian Peterson is now all but assured a spot in the Pro Football Hall of Fame when his time comes. He's almost guaranteed to become a Hall of Famer when the NFL announces the Class of 2026.

The hardest times in life have the potential to turn normal people into the strongest possible versions of themselves. No one should have to go through what Adrian Peterson went through. But if truly sad things in life do happen to you, let his story give you hope. So many people experience tragedies in life. In fact, everyone does. But it's what people do with the hardest times of their lives that helps shape them into who they'll ultimately become. Adrian Peterson chose to be the best version of himself while he played football. Choose to be the best version of yourself no matter what life throws at you!

· Had several unique nicknames while he played, including AD for "All Day," AP, and Purple Jesus.

· Idolized Emmitt Smith growing up.

· He became the first freshman in NCAA history to finish 2nd in the Heisman Trophy voting. This was the record before Texas A&M's Johnny Manziel won it as a freshman in 2012.

· Three-time NFL Rushing Champion (2008, 2012, 2015).

· A member of the NFL's 2010s All-Decade Team.

· Blew his knee out in 2011, but bounced back for an MVP season in 2012.

· Reached 10,000 rushing yards in just 101 games, the 3rd fastest to ever do it.

· Holds the record for most rushing touchdowns in a season.

· He has released his own rap music.

· One of the most approachable athletes. He regularly interacts with his fans in person and on social media.

1. Before Adrian Peterson broke the record, who was the player to reach 10,000 rushing yards the fastest?

2. How many rushing touchdowns did Adrian Peterson score to set the single-season rushing TD record?

3. AP may have played for the Vikings, but which team did he root for growing up?

4. Aside from football, what other sport is Adrian Peterson really good at?

5. True or false: Adrian Peterson won the Heisman Trophy while he played for Oklahoma.

6. What year was Adrian Peterson drafted?

7. True or false: He currently holds the most rushing yards in a single NFL game.

8. True or false: He has over 300 career catches.

9. How many teams has AP played for in his NFL career?

10. True or false: He was considering playing for the rival Texas Longhorns before deciding to play for Oklahoma.

ANSWER

1. *Jim Brown.*
2. *18.*
3. *The Dallas Cowboys.*
4. *Track.*
5. *False. He once finished second in Heisman voting but never won it.*
6. *2007.*
7. *True. 296 rushing yards is a single-game NFL record.*
8. *True! He has 305 career catches, showing he's more than just a great running back!*
9. *Seven teams! Vikings, Cardinals, Saints, Redskins, Lions, Titans, Seahawks.*
10. *True.*

"Adversity makes me hungrier. I thrive on being able to make a way out of no way."

"I remember my mistakes more than my success."

"If you don't think that you're the best, how do you become the best?"

"I have always believed that the way my parents disciplined me has a great deal to do with the success I have enjoyed as a man."

"I have the mentality that if you come in playing not to get hurt, that's when you're going to get hurt. So I play relentless."

LESSONS FROM STORY

· Have a role model you look up to who can guide you in life.

· Find something that brings you comfort in life, especially when you are sad.

· Set both realistic and ambitious goals for yourself, and then achieve them!

· Lean on your faith whenever you struggle in life.

· A good support system of true family and friends is everything!

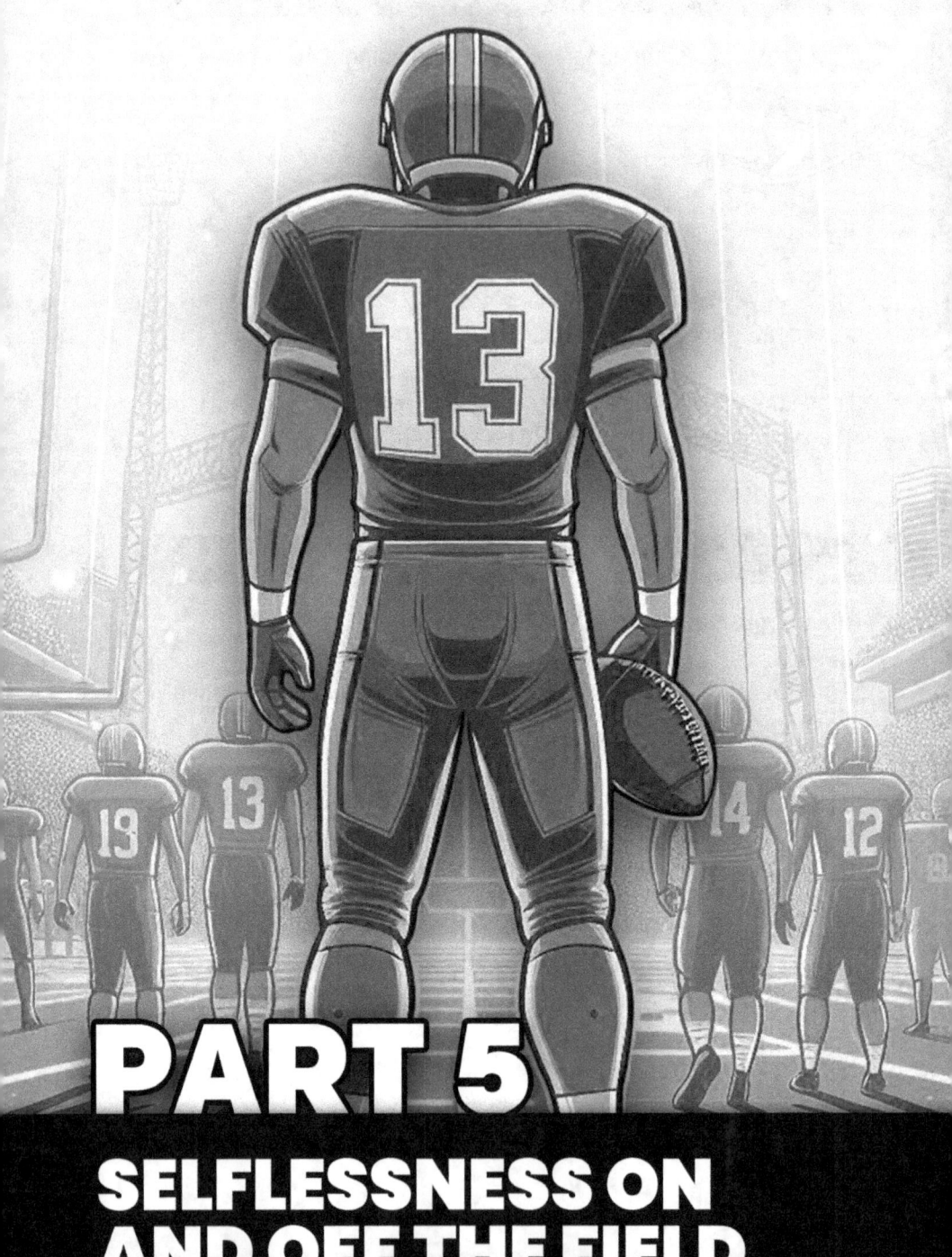

PART 5

SELFLESSNESS ON AND OFF THE FIELD

2002 TAMPA BAY BUCCANEERS
FROM WORST TO FIRST

For years after they were founded in 1974, the Tampa Bay Buccaneers were a joke. No one took them seriously. Every game that teams would play against them would be circled on the calendar as a guaranteed win. They even lost their first 26 games in a row! But after some success in the 1980s and 1990s, Bucs fans began expecting more from their team. They were tired of people calling their team the "Yucks." They were tired of losses early in the playoffs too. They finally wanted a taste of real gridiron glory.

Before the 2002 season, the Buccaneers traded a king's ransom for Raiders head coach Jon Gruden. They gave up two first round picks, two second round picks, and paid Oakland $8 million in cash. But once Gruden landed in Tampa Bay, it was clear that things were going to change for the better. Sometimes, a team doesn't need a pat on the shoulder.

Sometimes, what they need is a kick in the pants! Jon Gruden provided that for them. But before Gruden could get the team to buy in and perform well, he had to earn the respect of their star defensive end, Warren Sapp.

Sapp had been with the Bucs since they drafted him 12th overall in 1995, and was known for his fearsome ability as a pass rusher. But he was also known for being the vocal leader of the team. He was the alpha male. Sapp learned very quickly that Coach Gruden was the same way. While the Bucs' previous coach, Tony Dungy, was laid back and easygoing during practices, Gruden was the exact opposite. He wasn't afraid to get after the team if they weren't doing what they were supposed to do. "This guy had a full-fledged bite," Sapp said. "A venomous bite. You just couldn't sit still. And he used to always say, 'Bring juice to the practice field. And if you ain't got any juice, you're faking!'"

Not only was Gruden a strict coach who expected a lot from his team, he was also not afraid to surprise them by calling plays they weren't used to seeing in practice. Tampa Bay's defense thought that they were already one of the best in the NFL going into the 2002 season. But Gruden instantly showed them how much work they had to do.

On a practice drill that was normally a running play, Gruden called a pass play that instantly caught Sapp, linebacker Derrick Brooks, and safety John Lynch by surprise. He caught the three best players on the defense off guard. But more importantly, he had gained Warren Sapp's respect. "I looked him right in the eye, and I said, 'If you're scared, say you're scared,'" Sapp said.

Without missing a beat, Gruden turned around, stared his big 300-pound defensive leader down and barked, "Well it looks like they've been running that on you for three years! Now what?!" Jon Gruden was fearless. He was a no-nonsense head coach. Which is exactly who the Bucs needed. Gruden had gained Sapp's respect. He showed him who the boss was. Gruden challenged Sapp and the rest of the team to fully play up to their potential. And starting off the 2002 season, that's exactly what the Buccaneers did!

The team rolled to a surprising 5-1 start, led largely by their defense. Warren Sapp and his teammates were opportunistic. They forced a lot of turnovers, and ran them back for touchdowns whenever they could. Jon Gruden had his defense playing like they were the best in the NFL. But the offense was a different story. The unit, led by veteran quarterback Brad Johnson, was nearly outscored by the defense. Johnson and many of the Bucs' other offensive players had a hard time understanding Coach Gruden's complex strategy.

A lot of the names of the plays were coded and extremely hard to remember. It took over half the season for the Buccaneers' offense to get rolling. But once they got to Week 9 against the Minnesota Vikings, their offense finally roared to life! Brad Johnson threw for five touchdowns and 313 yards, and the Buccaneers rolled to a 38-24 win at home over Minnesota. But now the Bucs had to zero in and get focused for the rest of the season. And their focus could be summed up in just three words: pound the rock.

"Pound the rock" became the battle cry for Tampa Bay that season. Bucs offensive line coach Rod Marinelli came up with the term. Pound the rock didn't mean run the football. According to coach Jon Gruden, the saying meant something completely different: "The rock is the opponent, basically. You got to visualize yourself holding onto a hammer, and taking the best swings you can at that rock, trying to crack your opponent."

Someone on the coaching staff found an 80-pound slab of granite, and laid it down in the locker room. Every time Bucs players would walk in or out of the team facility, they'd be reminded of what they were supposed to do. And they would need that tough mentality, especially once they made it to the 2002 Playoffs.

The Buccaneers finished the regular season at 12-4 in 2002, good for the #2 seed in the NFC. The team rolled to a 31-6 win over the San Francisco 49ers in their first game. But in the NFC Championship, they'd have to get a massive monkey off their backs. The Philadelphia Eagles were the Bucs' version of the boogeyman. They had beaten Tampa Bay twice in the playoffs in 2000 and 2001. Not only that, they won again in the 2002 regular season as well.

Whenever the Bucs played the Eagles, Philly always seemed to have their number. Tampa would just seem to play timid, scared and look lost at Philadelphia's Veterans Stadium, while the Eagles would have a field day with them. But after three straight demoralizing losses to the Eagles, this NFC Championship Game would be different. The Bucs were ready to drag their boogeyman out from under the bed, and kick his butt!

Philadelphia took an early 7-0 lead, and looked like they were ready to haunt the Bucs yet again. But Tampa Bay would not be intimidated. A field goal and a long touchdown drive put them up 10-7. After the Eagles tied the game at 10 with a field goal, Tampa's defense took over. They stopped two Philly drives deep in Bucs territory while going ahead 20-10. And defensive back Ronde Barber delivered the knockout punch, as he took an interception back to the endzone to seal the game. The Bucs had finally defeated the Eagles. And they were now set to face the Oakland Raiders in Super Bowl 37.

Unlike the NFC Championship Game played the previous week against the Eagles, the Bucs were not scared of the Raiders at all. And it showed in how they played. This one wasn't even close. Tampa Bay's offense was solid. Brad Johnson threw two touchdown passes, and fullback Mike Alstott ran for a rushing touchdown. But the real star of the game, was the Buccaneer defense. They were completely locked in on Raiders quarterback Rich Gannon. They forced him into several bad mistakes, and made him pay for every single one.

The Bucs forced Gannon into throwing a Super Bowl record five interceptions. To make things even worse for Oakland, the Bucs returned three of the five interceptions for touchdowns to blow the game wide open. When the final whistle blew, the Buccaneers had destroyed the Raiders by a final score of 48-21. Jon Gruden, Warren Sapp, John Lynch, Derrick Brooks, and Brad Johnson had led their team to their first Super Bowl in franchise history. They were undisputed World Champions. The best football team on the planet. But more importantly, they showed what is possible when a team truly comes together and works toward a common goal.

If you play a team sport, or you're in a group project in school, it may not always be easy to get along with your classmates and teammates. Everyone has a different personality and different skills. But good teachers and coaches can make you and everyone else the best version of yourselves. If you have good teachers and coaches, listen to them! And once they've set out a clear goal for you all to accomplish, work together with each other to achieve it. Add your unique skills to the whole thing, but never put yourself above the team. If you are humble, hardworking, and willing to sacrifice for the good of your team, there is absolutely nothing that you can't accomplish. Just ask the 2002 Tampa Bay Buccaneers.

They turned a football team that everyone used to laugh at, into World Champions for the very first time. They were led by a tough but fair head coach, hungry leaders who stopped at nothing to win a Super Bowl, and every one of the 53 players on that team was willing to sacrifice everything in pursuit of their one common goal. And at the end of the line, they earned the right to hoist the greatest trophy in all of sports—the Lombardi Trophy!

· The team became the first to lead the league in total defense, points allowed and interceptions, since the 1985 Chicago Bears.

· The defense had four Hall of Famers on it: Warren Sapp, Derrick Brooks, Ronde Barber and John Lynch.

· Coach Jon Gruden said before the season that the team would need to return nine interceptions for touchdowns during the season if they wanted to win the Super Bowl. They had exactly that many...and won the Super Bowl!

· The Bucs' trade for Jon Gruden was one of the rare times a team traded for a head coach. Teams trading for a head coach instead of players doesn't usually happen, but it is possible.

· The Bucs beat the Raiders in the Super Bowl, Jon Gruden's former team. Gruden knew the Raiders inside and out, which probably gave Tampa Bay a big advantage in the big game!

· Even though the Bucs' defense was the best in the NFL in 2002, it took weeks for the offense to catch up. Most teams probably wouldn't have been able to handle that imbalance.

· Warren Sapp, Tampa's star defensive end, loved to joke around in practice with people he knew well. He was the class clown on the team. But when the time came to play football, he was all business!

· Sapp was originally supposed to go much higher in the 1995 NFL Draft. But he got into trouble with the law just before Draft Day, and he slid all the way down to the 12th pick, where Tampa took him.

· In every game of the 2002 season, the Bucs sacked the quarterback and forced at least one turnover. Talk about consistency!

· The Bucs had the lead going into the fourth quarter 10 times during the 2002 season, and never gave it up. The defense shut the game down every single time.

1. How many picks did the Buccaneers trade to get Jon Gruden?

2. How many weeks did it take for Tampa Bay to finally play their best football during the 2002 season?

3. What was Tampa Bay's team slogan in 2002?

4. True or false: This was Tampa Bay's first Super Bowl win ever.

5. The 2002 Tampa Bay Buccaneers were great at both passing and running the football.

6. True or False: The Buccaneers were one of only three teams who prevented opponents from scoring red zone touchdowns less than 40% of the time.

7. How many touchdowns did the Bucs allow in the month of October in 2002. Hint: It's really low.

8. True or false: The 2002 Buccaneers scored 35 points per game in the playoffs.

9. What was Bucs' quarterback Brad Johnson's nickname?

10. True or false: Brad Johnson was sacked 30 times.

ANSWER

1. *Two first round picks, two second round picks and $8 Million in cash!*
2. *Nine weeks.*
3. *Pound the Rock!*
4. *True!*
5. *False. Tampa Bay actually ranked 27th in rushing yards that year, and there were several games where they didn't get more than 75 rushing yards.*
6. *True!*
7. *Two touchdowns. They allowed only two total touchdowns in those four games, and the defense scored two touchdowns of their own!*
8. *True!*
9. *The Bull. He was nicknamed The Bull for how physically tough he was that season.*
10. *False. He was sacked 41 times in 2002. But he didn't make many mistakes!*

QUOTES

"As an athlete, that's what you dream of. That's what you want to do is get to a Super Bowl, win a Super Bowl. Not get to a Super Bowl, win it."

"We weren't supposed to get out of Philadelphia with a win and look at this? It's the best. It's the best thing that could have happened for us."

"At that moment, everything flashed before my eyes and then the celebrations started, 'We won this thing. We won it,"

"Rarely does a team alter the community it represents. This one did. It reached a deeper part of Tampa Bay than most teams do, even the most successful ones. The Bucs were suddenly a cool team to see, and Tampa Bay was a cool place to be."

"The birthplace of America is where the Bucs went to die each year. In 2002, they finally would come of age, thanks to the youngest coach in the NFL."

LESSONS FROM STORY

· Talent means nothing without hard work.

· Family can accomplish anything.

· It's good if you have a parent, teacher or some kind of leader to push you.

· True leaders step up and lead by example.

· If at first you don't succeed, try, try again. That's what the Bucs did against the Eagles until they finally defeated them.

JJ WATT

BIG PLAYS, BIGGER HEART

JJ Watt is now considered one of the best defensive ends of his generation. During his career, he racked up 114.5 sacks, and five Pro Bowl selections. But long before he ever became known for being Houston's game-breaking pass rusher, and every quarterback's worst nightmare, he was just a scrawny kid from Pewaukee, Wisconsin.

Watt had a blue-collar mindset instilled in him from an early age. His dad John Watt served nearly three decades in the Pewaukee Fire Department. He sometimes worked consecutive 24-hour shifts before coming home to spend time with JJ and his brothers TJ and Derek, while JJ's mother Connie worked as a building operations vice president. But JJ's biggest inspiration for his work ethic came from his paternal grandfather, James Watt. James was a Korean War veteran who served his country proudly. But he took pride in being a grandfather even more. He often drove the Watt brothers to football practice. And he was always right there rooting for all three brothers whether they played for the Pewaukee Pirates in high school or the Wisconsin Badgers in college. He was the loudest fan in the stands.

James Watt was also the one who taught JJ what it meant to be proud of his last name. And it was during one of the saddest times in JJ's life that he vowed to make his grandpa proud. As James was on his deathbed from cancer in February 2014, JJ realized what his grandpa meant to him. "I just tried to tell him how much we appreciate him. He was always there. His dad was an alcoholic, and he wasn't proud of the family name that he was handed down. So he worked his whole life to make his family name proud and to make it a name that meant something," JJ said. "That's what I told him on the last day. When I was holding his hand. I told him, 'We're going to make your name proud.'"

JJ certainly had the fuel and passion to make his grandpa proud. But the desire to do something, and making it happen are two very different things. JJ is now a future Hall of Famer. But getting to that point was anything but easy. Starting out in college, Watt wasn't a defensive end. He wasn't even at Wisconsin when his journey began. Coming out of Pewaukee High School, he was a two-star recruit, which meant he only got a handful of scholarships from smaller schools. So he chose to go to Central Michigan University and play in coach Butch Jones' system.

Watt thought he could make a big impact scoring touchdowns as a pass-catching tight end. But in 14 games for CMU, he only caught a total of eight passes for 77 yards. And after Butch Jones and his coaching staff wanted Watt to put on weight and become an offensive lineman instead, Watt turned Coach Jones down and decided to leave Central Michigan for Wisconsin. This was the first sign that JJ Watt wasn't just driven to be a fantastic football player, he also truly believed in himself and his dream. Football players who have scholarships very rarely give them up. And if they do, they don't go to one of the biggest schools in the country as a walk-on with no safety net. But JJ did that. He had the confidence to bet on himself. Plus, he wanted to go home to be closer to his family, and he wanted to pursue his chance at being a defensive end.

After he sat out for a season as a redshirt player, JJ put on weight and got even bigger and stronger. By the time he was in playing shape, he was absolutely massive! He stood at 6'5, and weighed 290 pounds! But you wouldn't know that he was that big by how fast he moved. In his first season, Watt was a freak of nature. He racked up 44 tackles, including 15.5 tackles for loss and 4.5 sacks. And he followed that up with a junior year where he became one of the top linemen in the nation!

In 2010, JJ stuffed the stat sheet. He racked up 62 total tackles, 21 tackles for loss, and 7.5 sacks. And he played so well that he was first team All-Big Ten, and a second team All-American. Following a fantastic finish to his college career, JJ did it again. He bet on himself. He skipped his senior year because he believed he was good enough to enter the NFL Draft. And once the Houston Texans took him #11 overall in 2011, he was proven right yet again. The blue-collar kid from Pewaukee, Wisconsin, didn't just open the door to his lifelong dream, he destroyed that door like he destroyed offensive lines!

JJ Watt had arrived, and had finally earned a chance to do what he always wanted to do. But as he would later say: "Heard someone say, 'I can't wait until I can finally say I made it.' The day you think you've 'made it' is the day you begin your decline."

Some people might not truly walk the walk. But that isn't JJ Watt. That's not who he is. When he played football, he was like the Energizer Bunny. He just kept going. He never stopped. Whether he was studying film, lifting, in practice, or playing on Sundays, the man only ever had one speed: FULL GO.

In his first season, Watt was a solid defensive player for Houston. But in just his second year in Year 2, he morphed into the NFL's best (and scariest) defensive player at just 23 years old. During that 2012 season, JJ Watt racked up 81 tackles, 16 pass breakups, four forced fumbles, and two fumble recoveries. But his crowning achievement that year was his mind-boggling 20.5 sacks. As a second-year player, Watt fell just 2.5 sacks shy of tying Hall of Famer Michael Strahan's single-season record. He was recognized as the NFL's Defensive Player of the Year for the first time in his career. Watt would tie his own personal best for sacks in 2014, and rack up 17.5 sacks in 2015. Both those years he was named to the Pro Bowl, and was the NFL's Defensive Player of the Year.

Later on in his career, JJ would struggle with injuries to his back, left leg, shoulder, and chest. He played eight games or less in 2016, 2017, 2019, and 2021 and retired in 2022 after two years with the Cardinals. But he's been inducted into the Houston Texans Ring of Honor, and he'll be likely to make it to the Hall of Fame in 2027 or 2028.

JJ Watt gave everything he had on the football field. Now that he's retired, he gives everything when it comes to helping others. He's the President and founder of the Justin J. Watt Foundation, which allows children in communities around the country to get involved in athletics in safe and fun ways. But the foundation has also helped people out during troubling times. When Hurricane Harvey hit Houston and the surrounding area, the Justin J. Watt Foundation raised a staggering $41.6 million in money that went toward relief efforts.

JJ Watt may now be world famous. But at his core, he's still the same bighearted, hardworking Wisconsin kid he's always been. He never forgot where he came from. And he never forgot how important it is to care about others more than himself. Those were lessons taught to him by John, Connie, and James Watt. And they're lessons that you can take from this story to use in your daily life.

No matter where you may be in your life, dream a big dream. And then once you know what your big dream is, set reachable goals and don't stop until you achieve them. And if you're fortunate enough to realize your lifelong dream like JJ Watt did, always remember to stay humble and put others before yourself. Love other people as equals. Don't look down on them. Even after you've reached the top, always treat them with respect and kindness.

Even though your dreams are important, the kindness that you show others will leave a legacy that will last long after you are grown up. JJ Watt's legacy is cemented both on and off the football field. Follow JJ's lead. Start working toward yours today. You can do it!

· He used to be a pizza delivery boy growing up.

· His celebrity crush is Jennifer Aniston.

· He's strong enough to flip over a tire that weighs 1,000 pounds!

· Instead of a mansion, JJ has a cabin and 35 acres of land in his home state of Wisconsin.

· JJ loves the TV show *Modern Family*.

· His favorite sport isn't football. It's actually hockey. JJ grew up in Wisconsin playing hockey for several years, until the cost of the gear and the skates became too much for his parents to afford. Then he switched to football and the rest is history!

· JJ is married to Kealia Ohai-Watt, a professional soccer player. They have a son together.

· Won the 2017 Walter Payton Man of the Year Award for his help in raising money for Hurricane Harve relief.

· He hosted *Saturday Night Live*.

· He was on the NFL's 2010s All-Decade Team

TRIVIA QUESTIONS

1. True or False: JJ Watt has been named the NFL Defensive Player of the Year twice.

2. JJ Watt is in the Pro Football Hall of Fame.

3. True or false: JJ Watt is also an actor.

4. How many career sacks does JJ Watt have?

5. How many times has JJ Watt been to the Pro Bowl?

6. True or False: JJ Watt has a Super Bowl ring.

7. True or false: JJ Watt runs his own charitable foundation to help kids.

8. True or False: Watt's two brothers, TJ Watt and Derek Watt, both played with JJ on the Texans.

9. How many sacks did JJ Watt get in 2012 to set the all-time sack record for the Houston Texans?.

10. True or false: JJ has appeared on the cover of *Sports Illustrated*.

ANSWER

1. False. He has won the award three times!
2. False. He's not in yet. He hasn't been retired for at least five years. But he very likely will be in the Hall of Fame very soon!.
3. True! He's appeared in shows like The League, New Girl and Ultimate Tag.
4. 114.5 sacks.
5. Five times.
6. False. He unfortunately never won a Super Bowl. But he's one of the NFL's greatest defensive players of all time!
7. True! He's the President of the Justin J. Watt Foundation, a foundation that helps kids get into athletics in a safe environment.
8. False. TJ and Derek played with each other on the Steelers, but they never played with JJ in Houstson.
9. 20.5 sacks
10. True! When an athlete makes it on the cover of that magazine, that usually means they've finally made it big!

QUOTES

"If you don't have that vision for the end goal, you have no clue where you're going, and you're going to work very hard to go nowhere."

"My whole life, I've been trying to make people proud."

"I'm going to continue to work to be the best player in the world, and whenever that doesn't sound fun to me anymore, that's when it's over."

"I never want to let a day go by without having done something to get a little better."

"My parents would definitely be my childhood heroes."

LESSONS FROM STORY

· Don't be afraid to bet on yourself. Don't do what others expect you to do, if it's not what you want.

· Your family name matters. Honor your parents by making something of yourself!

· Approach everything you do with passion!

· If you talk the talk, be prepared to back it up with your actions.

· Whether you become famous or not, always make sure to never forget where you came from. Give back to your community.

BERNIE KOSAR

HOMETOWN HERO

Most young kids often daydream about making winning plays for their favorite team while playing backyard football with their friends. But not many suit up years later and play as a quarterback for their favorite team. And even less people are actually good at it. Bernie Kosar played for his hometown Cleveland Browns from 1985 to 1993. His exploits on the field are legendary in Browns lore. But when you find out who he is, it makes his story even more impressive.

Bernie Kosar was born and raised in Youngstown, Ohio, 75 miles southeast of Cleveland and right on the Ohio-Pennsylvania border. Before Bernie was born, Youngstown, Cleveland, and the surrounding area were part of what was known as the Steel Belt. This area was the heart of steel production for the entire country. But when Bernie was growing up, the area became known as the Rust Belt when all the jobs disappeared. Bernie was part of a middle-class family, but he knew that he couldn't go to work in the steel mills and make good money like his father and grandfather used to do. His family also couldn't afford to send him to college. He didn't have many options, so he chose to stick with the one thing he loved to do: play football. "Football was your chance out," he said in an interview. "That was your family's chance for success."

But even if Bernie's family couldn't afford college, he was still determined to work hard in the classroom when he finally did get his chance to go to school. He was a star quarterback at the University of Miami, but he was also an incredibly hardworking student as well. On the field, he led the Hurricanes to their first National Championship in school history in 1983, when they upset heavily favored Nebraska to win it all. And he was just a 19-year-old freshman when he led the team to the top of the mountain!

Off the field, he double majored in Economics and Finance. He was extremely smart. Kosar played one more season at Miami in 1984, leading the team to an 8-5 record. But he knew that the 1985 and 1986 teams were going to be title contenders. He initially wanted to stay in South Florida and try to win another National Championship. But then the chance to go pro, and the desire to take care of his family tugged at his heart. He had to go pro right then, and he knew it. He was going to be a football star in the NFL. He could see it. Being an NFL quarterback would be his way to provide and care for his family back home in Youngstown.

But then Bernie did something that is incredibly rare for any NFL player. He openly pushed for a chance to play for his favorite team: the Cleveland Browns. He grew up rooting for the Browns as a boy in the 1960s and 1970s. The opportunity to chase a lifelong dream was right in front of him. It was so close. Bernie wanted to pull on that brown and orange jersey so badly!

The Browns knew how much Bernie wanted to play for them. So they made a big trade. They traded four picks, including two first rounders, to the Buffalo Bills. That allowed Bernie to skip the 1985 NFL Draft in April, and the Browns took him in the supplemental draft in the summer of 1985. He was home!

The boy from Youngstown, Ohio, who had grown up loving the Cleveland Browns was now a member of the team. And after sitting behind veteran quarterback Gary Danielson for the first half of the 1985 season, Bernie became a starter in the NFL when Danielson went down with an injury. Kosar never looked back.

The Browns finished that season 8-8, but Bernie had led them to the playoffs. And from that point on, that was the expectation. The Browns expected to win. And they won a lot. After the 1985 season they continued their run. They made the playoffs every year from 1986 to 1989. But what made the run so special wasn't just that the Browns finally had a great quarterback. Bernie led the offense in a unique but effective way.

When you think of a fantastic quarterback who do you see in your mind? You probably think of Tom Brady, Peyton Manning, Ben Roethlisberger, or somebody else like that. Big guys who can throw perfect passes and look good while doing it. Bernie Kosar was the exact opposite. Experts often described Bernie as an "ugly duckling." He was extremely tall at 6'5. But he was skinny at just 215 pounds. He was also one of the slowest quarterbacks around. And to top it all off, when Bernie threw the ball, he didn't throw it like a normal quarterback. He often threw the ball with a goofy-looking sidearm motion. If the NFL had style points, Bernie wouldn't have gotten any. He wasn't athletic. At all. But what Bernie didn't have in terms of talent or athletic ability, he made up for with toughness, courage, and was a genius at understanding how defenses worked. He was incredibly smart and gutsy.

While most quarterbacks would probably panic as soon as the defense started pressuring them, Bernie never did. In fact, his calm attitude under pressure made him dangerous to defenses. Even downright deadly. Bernie would read the defense extremely well before snapping the football, adjust the offense as needed, and then stand in the pocket until the last possible second before delivering the throw. Most of the time, his receivers caught the ball for a huge gain or a touchdown. But this also led to Bernie getting hit hard by the defense. However, Bernie's courage under pressure made him inspiring to many in Cleveland.

Bernie was now truly a hometown hero. The tough guy. He was the leader of a blue-collar football team that made the people of Cleveland proud and happy by winning a lot of games on Sundays. But most importantly, he was now taking care of his family, just as he set out to do.

Bernie led the Browns to the playoffs five times during his career and won four AFC Central titles. But sadly, he never appeared in or won a Super Bowl with the Browns. He came very close to going to the Super Bowl a couple times, particularly in 1986 and 1987, but both times, the Browns suffered heartbreaking losses to John Elway and the Denver Broncos in the AFC Championship Game. However, Bernie didn't throw in the towel. He continued to play for the Browns until the 1993 season. By that point though, he was 30 years old, and nine years of hard hits, sacks, and concussions began to take their toll on his body. He eventually retired from football in 1996 at the age of 33 after finishing out his career with the Cowboys and Dolphins. He finally won a Super Bowl ring in 1993 with Dallas as a backup quarterback, but his football home will always be in Cleveland.

Bernie Kosar never won a Super Bowl with his hometown Browns. And he's not a Hall of Famer. But in the eyes of Browns fans, he's something greater: He's theirs. He's one of them. Bernie grew up seeing the hard times the city of Cleveland had gone through, and simply wanted to make a difference. He wanted to lift the city up. He wanted to make people smile. Playing football was his way of doing that.

"When I came to the Browns, our area was still the butt of national jokes," Bernie said. "The Cuyahoga River caught on fire. The city was bankrupt. The unemployment. In Miami, I heard all that. I shrugged it off, but it bothered me. I kept thinking I could go back there and do something about all the negative stuff. I could help my family have security, and I could play for my favorite team. This was a childhood dream and I could make people happy who loved the Browns."

Bernie Kosar did all that and more for Northeast Ohio. Cleveland is often jokingly referred to as the "Mistake on the Lake." But when he led the Browns in his best years, that football team gave people hope. And it all started when a native son decided to go home to Ohio from sunny Miami. And because of his choice to come home, and his incredible effort once he stepped onto the field for the Browns, Bernie Kosar will be loved in Cleveland forever. Even long after he is gone.

You may or may not be a star football player like Bernie Kosar was. But you can still imitate his toughness and determination. What hurdles do you need to work harder to overcome as you grow up? You can imitate Bernie's selflessness by helping your own community too! He played football to lift people up. But you can volunteer at a homeless shelter, soup kitchen, or donate to help those who have fallen on hard times. Take a cue from Bernie himself and lift others up. He lifted people up through football. Lift others up in your own unique and special way.

· He initially wanted to stay in Ohio and play college football for Ohio State. But the coach thought he looked weird throwing the football, and didn't recruit him.

· Education is very important to Bernie. He worked hard and graduated from the University of Miami a year and a half early.

· He now serves as an advocate for other former football players who have suffered concussions like he has, and pushes for the NFL to make football safer.

· Was Ohio's Division I high school Player of the Year in 1981.

· Attended Youngstown Boardman High School.

· He played both football and baseball in high school.

· Led the University of Miami to their first National Championship in football in 1983, when the Hurricanes upset heavily favored Nebraska in the 1984 Orange Bowl Game.

· Made his lone Pro Bowl appearance in 1986, when he led the Browns to one of their best records in their history. They won 12 games and came within five minutes of appearing in Super Bowl 21.

· He's broken bones in both hands, and several other bones from all the hits he took during his playing career.

· He now routinely appears on several Cleveland-area podcasts and shows, sharing stories from his playing days with the fans. He's a very visible public figure. Even at 60 years old!

1. True or False: Bernie Kosar was an extremely athletic quarterback when he played.

2. True or false: Bernie Kosar once held an NFL record for the most passes without throwing an interception.

3. How many picks did the Browns trade in order to draft Bernie Kosar?

4. True or False: Bernie was taken first overall in the 1985 NFL Draft.

5. True or false: The Houston Oilers were so angry about not getting a chance to draft Bernie in the regular Draft, that they threatened to sue the NFL and stop the NFL Draft.

6. True or False: Bernie Kosar led the Browns to the Playoffs in his rookie season at just 22 years old.

7. True or false: Bernie Kosar was sacked 200 times in his career.

8. True or False: Bernie Kosar won a Super Bowl ring with the Browns.

9. True or false: Bernie Kosar has written a book about his playing days, as well as dealing with the lasting injuries he's suffered during his career.

10. True or false: Bernie Kosar has four children.

ANSWER

1. False!

2. True! He once threw a remarkable 308 passes in a row without being intercepted!

3. They traded a whopping four draft picks, including two first round picks, to get him to Cleveland with Buffalo's first pick.

4. False. He was taken first in something called the Supplemental Draft, which was for players who did not wish to enter the regular NFL Draft.

5. True!

6. True!

7. False: He was sacked 250 times. This led to numerous concussions and injuries.

8. False. But he DID win a Super Bowl ring as a backup quarterback with the Dallas Cowboys in 1993.

9. True. He wrote an autobiography titled Learning to Scramble.

10. True! His children's names are Sara, Rebecca, Rachel and Joseph, with Bernie often crediting his daughter Sara with helping him get healthy and take better care of himself since she's a yoga instructor.

"I wasn't mechanically the best quarterback. But in the heat of the battle, you can't be thinking about mechanics. The ball's just gotta come out the way it naturally comes out."

"I always try to take a negative and turn it into a positive. I don't like to dwell on the bad things. I don't like to feel sorry for myself, and I don't like excuses for failure."

"When they were blitzing, instead of playing it safe, that was my chance to go for a home run and score a touchdown. So when I saw the all-out blitz coming, no matter when it was, where it was, I was taking a shot."

"He was the typical guy that the city would fall in love with. Not John Elway. Not a great athlete. But smart, hardworking, courageous and maximizing his ability. The city went nuts."

"What are your gifts that God's given you? What are your limitations? What could you do, what can't you do? I had to take advantage mentally of every situation I could take advantage of. Find a way, somehow some way. Find a way to get it done."

LESSONS FROM STORY

· Find what you are good at, and what makes you happy.

· Find ways to lift others up using your gifts.

· Work hard to overcome any obstacles or shortcomings that you have.

· Education and learning is extremely important to success.

· Hard work, heart and courage can overcome a lack of talent.

REGGIE WHITE

THE MINISTER OF DEFENSE

Reggie White earned the nickname "The Minister of Defense" in 1983, and it stuck with him for the rest of his life. He was a unique man. On one side of things, he was a quarterback's worst nightmare. He was a mountain of a man who stood 6'5, weighed 300 pounds, and took joy in terrorizing opposing offenses every Sunday. But off the football field, he had a softer side. He was a deeply faith-filled man with a heart full of compassion for others. He was a devout Christian who was concerned with helping his fellow man, and preaching the Gospel wherever he could. Let's dive into this gentle giant's legacy!

Some football players stumble into their passion and destiny by accident. Others know that they're destined for gridiron glory at an early age. Reggie White was one of them. At 12 years old in 1973, he told his mother that he wanted to do two things: play football and be a minister. And he did just that. At 17 years old, he became an ordained minister, and at Howard High School in his hometown of Chattanooga, Tennessee, he immediately received national attention for how well he played on the field. He racked up 140 tackles, 10 sacks, and was named a high school All-American in 1979. He was destined for football stardom, and he knew it. As soon as he arrived at the University of Tennessee, Reggie was solid through his first three years playing for the Volunteers. But his senior year in 1983 truly showed the force of nature he would become.

After coming off a nagging ankle injury in 1982, White's football fury was unleashed. He racked up an eye-popping 100 tackles and 15 sacks, which is a single season record for Tennessee football. Professional football teams soon began scrambling to pick up the massive defensive end. He initially signed with the Memphis Showboats of the United States Football League and spent his first two professional seasons in his home state. But once the USFL collapsed, the Philadelphia Eagles signed Reggie to an initial four-year deal. But he ended up playing there until 1992. During his time with the Birds from 1985 to 1992, White and his teammate and best friend Jerome Brown, were the leaders of one of the most fearsome defenses in NFL history!

To put it bluntly, Reggie White was a sack machine at this point in his career. His most productive season came in 1987. The NFL season that year was shortened to 12 games because of a player's strike. But Reggie still managed to rack up an incredible 21 sacks. He was so good that season with the Eagles that he was named the Defensive Player of the Year!

The Philadelphia defense was Super Bowl-worthy. But unfortunately, the Eagles never won a Super Bowl. Emmitt Smith, Troy Aikman, Michael Irvin, and the division-rival Cowboys were just too strong for the Eagles to overcome, as Dallas won a Super Bowl near the end of Reggie's time as an Eagle in 1992. But even though Reggie White is now probably remembered for playing as a member of the Green Bay Packers, he never wanted to leave Philadelphia. He loved the city, and he loved playing with his best friend, Jerome Brown.

However, once Jerome tragically passed away from a car accident in 1992, and Eagles owner Norman Braman refused to sign Reggie White to an extension, Reggie decided to go to the Green Bay Packers as a free agent. While he was in Green Bay, Reggie was just as effective there as he had been in Philadelphia. He was a downright monster! Reggie played there for six seasons, racked up 68.5 sacks, and even helped Brett Favre and his Packers teammates win a Super Bowl in 1997!

In that game, White played like an absolute madman. He made Patriots quarterback Drew Bledsoe run for his life all game long. And when Bledsoe couldn't get away, Reggie brought him down hard. The Minister of Defense had three sacks, including one to seal the victory at the very end of the game. He finally had a Super Bowl ring to match his unbelievable dominance on the field.

Reggie White retired from football in 2000. When all was said and done, he was a 13-time Pro Bowler, two-time Defensive Player of the Year, Super Bowl Champion, and was the all-time leader in sacks with 198. Not only that, but he also recorded well over a thousand tackles. He simply had a "sixth sense" when it came to finding the football or sacking the quarterback. However, for as great of a football player Reggie White was on the field, he was an even better man off it. And this all stemmed from his deep faith in Jesus Christ. White once said, "People consider me a success because I'm a good football player and make lots of money. But if my heart's not right, if I'm not living a life pleasing to God, I'm a failure."

This perspective on life shaped all that Reggie did. It was even why he became a Green Bay Packer in 1993. While most free agents are concerned about money, being on a winning team, or getting more playing time, Reggie White chose Green after his time in Philadelphia because he felt he could pursue his other calling: helping those in need. White even told prospective teams that he preferred playing in a city where he could minister to, and help other people.

Just like he did in Philadelphia, Reggie helped those who needed it the most in Green Bay. He wanted to do it in any way that he could. "People will say I went for the money, and the money does have something to do with it. But it gives me the opportunity to build businesses, create housing and create opportunities for the people of the inner city. I want to do that all over the country."

White did everything. He preached the Gospel on street corners, generously donated his money to several charitable organizations, and spent time with those who were struggling in the inner city. He was also a member of the Fellowship of Christian Athletes or FCA, and used his platform to uplift others since he was a celebrity. But just as he was set to truly make a massive impact during his retirement, he passed away suddenly in 2004. He was 43 years old. However, even though he's physically gone, his legacy and spirit endure forever.

During his induction into the Pro Football Hall of Fame in 2006, his widow Sara White, reminded all those in attendance, that remembering Reggie and living by his example would keep his memory alive forever: "One last thing. We're talking about history. We knew Reggie, Reggie's history in football. Just like Jeremy said, Reggie's legacy will live on through you. If you continue to do what you need to do, and your family first, your community, your school, at your work job, your legacy, you would take Reggie's spirit and legacy with you because that's what he would want you to do."

You all have dreams that you want to accomplish. And chasing those dreams is a noble goal. But how can you chase your dreams, while giving back to others who may not be as fortunate as you are? Do you volunteer, spend time with the people society ignores, or live your life the way Reggie White lived his? We can have all the success in the world in whatever we choose to do, but like Reggie said, if our hearts aren't in the right place, we risk failing. We fail those who need our help the most and we fail ourselves.

If you have some free time, take the time to go out of your comfort zone. Approach the kid who looks lonely at lunch and sit down and talk to them. Sit next to a classmate you may not know, and say hi to them and be their friend. Volunteer your time on a weekend helping a homeless shelter instead of staying in and playing video games or doing your usual activities. If you do all these things, you're living like Reggie White lived his life. And you're making him proud. The Minister of Defense may have been a big man, but off the football field, he was simply Reginald Howard White. And he had an even bigger heart!

· He studied the Torah extensively even though he was a Christian.

· He could speak fluent Hebrew.

· The Packers and Eagles both retired his #92 jersey after he passed away.

· At the time of his retirement, he led the NFL in sacks with 198, a record that has since been broken.

· He is a member of both the Pro Football Hall of Fame and the College Football Hall of Fame.

· During his playing career with both the Packers and Eagles, Reggie White was a member of the NFL's 1980s and 1990s All-Decade Teams.

· Surprisingly, Reggie was a relative unknown when he started playing college football at Tennessee.

· Reggie White so far is the only NFL player ever, to have 20 or more sacks in just 12 games in a season. He did that in 1987 for the Eagles.

· In 1987, he also set an NFL record by averaging almost two sacks a game for the entire season.

· He became an ordained Baptist minister during his Sophomore year at Tennessee.

1. True or false: Reggie White is a member of four different Halls of Fame.

2. Do you remember Reggie White's famous nickname? What is it?

3. How many times did Reggie White win Defensive Player of the Year?

4. True or false: Reggie White was named to the Pro Bowl 13 straight seasons.

5. What numbers did Reggie White wear?

6. True or false: Reggie White won two Super Bowls.

7. True or false: He went straight from Tennessee to the NFL.

8. True or false: The Tennessee Volunteers, Philadelphia Eagles and Green Bay Packers all retired Reggie White's #92.

9. How many consecutive seasons did Reggie White have where he racked up at least nine sacks?

10. How many seasons did Reggie White have where he racked up at least 15 or more sacks?

ANSWER

1. True! He is a member of both the Pro and College Football Halls of Fame, the Wisconsin Athletic Hall of Fame, and the Philadelphia Sports Hall of Fame.
2. The Minister of Defense.
3. Twice.
4. True! He was named a Pro Bowler from 1986-1998.
5. He wore both #91 and #92.
6. False. He only won one Super Bowl.
7. False. He played the first two seasons of his professional career with the Memphis Showboats of the United States Football League (USFL) in 1984 and 1985.
8. True.
9. 10 straight seasons. Unbelievable!
10. Two seasons.

"People consider me a success because I'm a good football player and make lots of money. But if my heart's not right, if I'm not living a life pleasing to God, I'm a failure."

"I have a lot of respect for tough coaches."

"God does not call the equipped. He equips the called."

"Success is not defined by what you accomplish, but by the obstacles you overcome."

"Strength does not come from physical capacity."

LESSONS FROM STORY

· Use whatever platform and talent you have to lift up and glorify God's name.

· It's okay to be a late bloomer.

· Help those who aren't as fortunate as you are.

· Go out of your way to be kind and welcoming to others you wouldn't normally meet or talk to.

· Approach school and your hobbies with intensity, but be kind and gentle when you're interacting with others.

BARRY SANDERS

HUMILITY IN ACTION

The touchdown dance is one of the most iconic things in professional football. There have been hundreds, if not thousands, of different touchdown dances over the years. Some are cool, others are funny, and a few of them are just downright weird. But for the greatest running back in the history of the Detroit Lions, he always did the same thing after he reached the endzone. After every one of his 100 career rushing touchdowns, Barry Sanders always calmly and respectfully flipped the ball back to the referee before running back to the sidelines with his teammates. He always acted like he had been there before. He never showed off. Since he's one of the greatest running backs in NFL history, he never had to show off. Barry let his play on the field do the talking for him. But the ball flip was more than just Sanders being humble. It's who he truly is as a person.

Barry was one of 11 children born to William and Shirley

Sanders in Wichita, Kansas. William was a hardworking man who was also a strict father, while Shirley was the quiet, loving, nurturing mother to her children. As he grew older, Barry would learn hard work and perseverance from his father, while looking like and acting like his mother. He was a quiet boy growing up.

Although it may seem harsh by today's standards, William Sanders would often tell his sons and daughters, "I'm not your friend. I'm your father." But he often showed his love for his children instead of saying it. One of the ways that William showed his love for Barry was to stick up for him when he played football. William Sanders was never one to brag about his son in public. He would often lift up the team instead. But William would often stick up for his Barry when he felt the team wasn't using him properly. The first example of this was when Barry played high school football at Wichita North High School.

Barry was considered undersized back then, and his high school coach also thought he was afraid of contact. So he played Barry at cornerback instead. This didn't sit well with William Sanders, who heavily criticized the coaching staff. "I'm not talking about Coach Shepler," William said angrily. "He didn't play it right. He didn't think Barry would be a great running back. He wouldn't play Barry at running back."

While his father was upset with the coach, Barry was concerned about something else: college offers. By this point, he was in his junior year of high school, and hadn't received a single letter to play for any college. Barry might not have had any scholarship offers, but that still didn't stop him from working out hard to get in shape. He frequently helped his dad with construction jobs, which sculpted his body into top physical condition. And before he knew it, Barry had a new coach leading the team his senior year, and he was finally going to play running back.

When Barry got the chance to run with the football for the first time, he took off! He rushed for over 1,400 yards as a senior in 1985, averaged an incredible 10 yards per carry, and began to show glimpses of the running style that he would become famous for. He had the talent to stop and start while he was running, make defenders miss, and change direction in a split second. Surprisingly, he still didn't get many college offers. The only colleges who were interested in recruiting Barry at the time were Tulsa, and Oklahoma State. Barry's father strongly tried to push him toward playing at Tulsa. He would get immediate playing time as a starting running back with the Golden Hurricane. But Barry fell in love with Oklahoma State and immediately signed on to play with the Cowboys. His path to stardom wouldn't be easy though. Oklahoma State already had an All-American running back named Thurman Thomas.

He may not have been the starting running back for his first two years in college, but Barry took advantage of every opportunity he did get. He primarily returned punts and kickoffs in 1986 and 1987, and flashed his elusiveness and world class speed. In fact, he was so good on special teams, he was the nation's top kick returner in 1987! But 1988 would truly be an incredible season. That would be Barry's final season with Oklahoma State, and he would end his college career with a bang! Opposing defenses were chasing him all season long, as he ran for over 2,600 yards and scored a whopping 39 touchdowns. Once Barry started running, he didn't stop running until he had claimed the Heisman Trophy as the best college football player in America!

Most players in Barry's position would absolutely love all the attention that comes with being crowned the Heisman winner. Especially if they knew they were going to be a top draft pick. But he hated it. He was grateful to win the award, but he felt unworthy of it. One thing he was worthy of though was being taken by the Detroit Lions with the third overall pick in the 1989 NFL Draft.

When he landed in Detroit, Barry picked up right where he left off, as he gave a spark to a Lions team that had only won four games in 1988. The team still missed the playoffs with a 7-9 record in 1989, but Barry had a fantastic season. He ran for nearly 1,500 yards and 14 touchdowns on his way to Rookie of the Year! But since Barry was playing really well, that also meant that people were paying more and more attention to him. Barry was a certified NFL superstar. But he never quite got comfortable with being the face of the Lions or doing postgame interviews. Barry was more comfortable when he was able to meet people naturally in the Detroit community, or teach kids through football camps. Barry had big-time talent, but he had the quiet, humble personality of a small-town guy.

However, just because he was quiet and humble didn't mean that he wasn't a nightmare for opposing defenses! Over the course of his 10 seasons in the NFL from 1989 to 1998, Sanders was named a Pro Bowler six times, a first or second team All-Pro selection every season of his career, he averaged 100 yards rushing per game, and was named the NFL's Most Valuable Player in 1997.

Barry played one more season for the Lions in 1998 before deciding to retire at just 30 years old. He passionately loved the game of football and the city of Detroit during his best years, but he gave absolutely everything he had to the point where he eventually no longer felt the joy for the game like he once did. He worked himself so hard that he'd burned out. Not to mention, the Lions only won a single playoff game during Barry's 10-year career. They never got closer to the Super Bowl than an ugly loss to the Washington Redskins in the 1991 NFC Championship Game. The wear and tear of being a running back in the NFL took its toll on Barry. Not to mention the Lions suffered heartbreaking playoff losses year after year.

Even though he didn't have the postseason success that he wanted, he is still one of the very few players who are in the discussion for the greatest running back in NFL history. And his legacy is forever cemented as a Pro Football Hall of Famer. There's no doubt about it. Barry Sanders is one of the most talented and gifted football players to ever live. But he did so much more than just rely on his talent to get him to the Hall of Fame. He stayed humble, kept his nose clean, served as a role model on and off the field for kids in Detroit and all across America, and never forgot where he came from.

No matter what kind of talents you have, always stay humble and kind to others. Work as hard as you can and give back when you can in how you help other people. Barry Sanders may be a football legend. But more than anything else, he is known as a good man. You may end up becoming very successful in whatever you do. But above all, take a cue from Barry Sanders: Stay humble and always strive to be a good person.

· The Detroit Lions retired his #20 jersey on November 25th, 2004, and inducted him into the Pride of the Lions, the team's Hall of Fame.

· He was inducted into the Pro Football Hall of Fame at just 36 years old, becoming the second youngest member in history.

· His son, who goes by Barry J. Sanders, played college football for both Stanford and Oklahoma State. But he chose not to play pro football after college. He works for Electronic Arts or EA, a big-time video game company.

· Played college football for Oklahoma State.

· Won the Heisman Trophy in 1988.

· Played in the NFL for nine seasons from 1989-1998.

· Was named the NFL MVP in 1997.

· Was named a Pro Bowler in every season of his career.

· His yards per carry average is an astounding 5.0.

· Was well known for his shifty running style. He would run side to side to find openings, while many running backs would run straight ahead.

1. What was Barry Sanders' touchdown celebration whenever he scored?

2. True or false: The Lions only won one playoff game in Barry Sanders' career.

3. True or false: Barry loved the attention he'd get from the media and the fans.

4. True or false: Barry Sanders and his dad William, were polar opposite in terms of personality.

5. How many rushing touchdowns did Barry Sanders score in his career?

6. True or false: Barry Sanders is in the Top 5 on the NFL's all-time rushing leaders list.

7. When was Barry Sanders inducted into the Pro Football Hall of Fame?

8. Why did Barry Sanders leave the NFL?

9. True or false: Barry Sanders loved getting involved in the Detroit community.

10. True or False: His son goes by Barry Sanders Jr.

ANSWER

1. He didn't celebrate touchdowns. All he did was flip the football back to the referee and run back to the sidelines.
2. True.
3. False. He appreciated his fans, but he hated the attention. He's a very private, quiet person.
4. True. William Sanders was always way more outspoken than his son.
5. 99 rushing touchdowns.
6. True. He's 4th on the all-time rushing list with 15,269 rushing yards.
7. 2004.
8. He was frustrated with Lions management.
9. True! Even though he was a quiet, private person, he loved meeting new people away from the cameras and spotlight.
10. False. Barry's son goes by Barry James Sanders, to avoid confusion with his dad.

"Nothing ever turns out the way people expect it to."

"Maybe a good rule in life is to never become too important to do your own laundry."

"Life doesn't stop with football."

"Happiness doesn't come from football awards. Happiness comes from a good job, being able to feed your wife and kids."

"I don't dream football. I dream the American Dream. Two cars in a garage, and being a happy father."

LESSONS FROM STORY

· Stay humble no matter how successful you are. Act like you've been there before.

· Work as hard as you can, and give back to your community when you can.

· Keep trying your best at whatever you do, even if success doesn't happen right away.

· Never forget where you come from, no matter how successful you become.

· Do what's right for you, even if people disagree with you.

REFERENCES

(2) NFL on X: "Four months ago, Damon Sheehy-Guiseppi was sleeping outside because he couldn't afford a hotel. He talked his way into a contract with the @Browns and today he scored an 86-yard punt return TD! What. A. Moment. @damon015 https://t.co/apiNylE7Wn"

10 fun and interesting Al Davis facts—10-facts-about.com

131 Adrian Peterson Facts: Career, Childhood, Accomplishments, and More—Kidadl

3 Interesting Facts about NFL Hall of Famer Emmitt Smith—familysearch.org

30 for 30 | The Minister of Defense Excerpt | Brett Favre on Reggie White—youtube.com

A Football Life - Reggie White & Jerome Brown HD—youtube.com

A Football Life Barry Sanders—youtube.com

A Football Life Emmitt Smith—youtube.com

A Football Life Jerome Bettis—youtube.com

A Football Life: LaDainian Tomlinson—youtube.com

A Football Life Cris Carter—youtube.com

A Look Back at the Raiders' Emotional Win Over the Texans in 2011 | NFL Throwback | Raiders— youtube.com

About JJ (jjwfoundation.org)

Adrian Peterson plays through pain of son's death—CNN

Adrian Peterson Witnessing 9-Year-Old Brother's Horrific Death Is Just 1 of Multiple Tragedies He Overcame—sportscasting.com
Adrian Peterson: Brother Killed by Drunk Driver—youtube.com

America's Game 2002 Tampa Bay Buccaneers—youtube.com

Barry Sanders Facts for Kids—kiddle.co

Bernie Kosar Tried to Get Browns to Draft TE Jimmy Graham—Dawgs By Nature

America's Game 2002 Tampa Bay Buccaneers—youtube.com

Barry Sanders Facts for Kids—kiddle.co

Bernie Kosar Tried to Get Browns to Draft TE Jimmy Graham—Dawgs By Nature

Best of Cris Carter's Pro Football Hall of Fame speech—youtube.com

Browns WR Damon Sheehy-Guiseppi's Amazing Journey to the NFL | Full Interview | The Rich Eisen Show—youtube.com

Chuck Pagano Facts for Kids—kiddle.co

Coach Pagano Emotional Post-Game Speech After Colts Win [HD]—youtube.com

Colts 28-16 Texans (Dec 30, 2012) Game Recap—ESPN

Cris Carter College Stats, School, Draft, Gamelog, Splits | College Football at Sports—Reference.com

Cris Carter Facts for Kids—kiddle.co

Damon Sheehy-Guiseppi, the Rookie Who Was Previously Homeless, Has Been Released by Browns—CBSSports.com

Deaf NFL Players: Inspiring Athletes—AI-media

E 60 -J J Watt Full Feature (broken down)—youtube.com

Emmitt Smith, Hall of Fame Speech (2010)—youtube.com

Former Colts HC Chuck Pagano Tells Pat McAfee About Coaching with Leukemia—youtube.com

From 2-Star to Superstar: J.J. Watt's Football Career is a Story of Perseverance—FanBuzz

From NFL Coach to Fighting Leukemia: Chuck Pagano's Story—youtube.com

Gladys Bettis Breast Cancer Research Foundation—BCRF

Gold Jacket Spotlight: Emmitt Smith Turned Dreams to Goals the 'Write' Way | Pro Football

Hall of Fame—profootballhof.com

How the 1968 New York Jets Changed NFL History—BVM Sports

"I Guarantee It" 1969: Joe Namath—The Pop History Dig

J.J. Watt of Houston Texans Treasures Last Name to Honor Grandfather—Houston Texans Blog- ESPN

J.J. Watt's Family: 5 Fast Facts You Need to Know (heavy.com)

Jerome Bettis' Family: 5 Fast Facts You Need to Know—heavy.com

Jerome Bettis Says He Sold Drugs and Shot at People While Growing Up in Detroit | News, Scores, Highlights, Stats, and Rumors—Bleacher Report

Jimmy Graham Is a Pilot, Sailing around the World, a Racecar Driver, & Probably Most Interesting NFL—youtube.com

Jimmy Graham's Top Plays w/ New Orleans Saints (2010-2014)—youtube.com

Jimmy Graham's Unlikely Path—youtube.com

Joe Namath: A Football Life - The Guarantee—youtube.com

LaDainian Tomlinson turns 44: 5 Things You May Not Have Known about the Hall of Fame RB—CBSSports.com

Larry Brown Highlights—youtube.com

Larry Brown Stats, Height, Weight, Position, Draft, College—Pro-Football-Reference.com

Larry Brown, the Unlikeliest Washington Redskins Star—riggosrag.com

Legendary Saints kicker Tom Dempsey dies at 73—nfl.com

Raiders 25-20 Texans (Oct 9, 2011) Game Recap—ESPN

Razorbacks | Brandon Burlsworth Foundation—Harrison

Reggie White | Pro Football Hall of Fame—profootballhof.com

Reggie White Dies at 43—packers.com

Roger Staubach Explains How he Coined 'Hail Mary' Phrase—sportsnaut.com

Saints legend Tom Dempsey (NO Club QB)—youtube.com

Shaquem Griffin Facts for Kids—kiddle.co

The Autumn Wind—youtube.com

The Dreams, the Decision and the Pressure: Bernie Kosar's Story of Becoming a Cleveland Brown – Terry Pluto—cleveland.com

The Heartbreaking Story of the Greatest Walk-On Ever, Brandon Burlsworth | College GameDay—youtube.com

The Improbable Story of How Little Known WR Damon Sheehy-Guiseppi Landed a Tryout and, Ultimately, a Contract with the Browns—clevelandbrowns.com

The Incredible Story of Shaquem Griffin | SC Featured | ESPN—youtube.com

The Legend of Browns QB Bernie Kosar (Complete Story)—brownsnation.com)

The Life and Career of Reggie White (Complete Story)—profootballhistory.com

The Life and Still-Impactful Legacy of Brandon Burlsworth—FOX Sports

The Story of the Original Hail Mary! | Legends of the Playoffs—youtube.com
The Watt Brothers (youtube.com)

Tom Dempsey NFL Films Feature—youtube.com

Tom Dempsey, Record-Setting NFL Kicker, Dies from Coronavirus at 73— sandiegouniontribune.com

Top 10 Quotes by Reggie White—azquotes.com

Top 15 Things You Didn't Know About J.J. Watt—thesportster.com

What Happened to Brandon Burlsworth? Everything You Need to Know—YEN.COM.GH

What Happened to Jimmy Graham? (His Unfortunate Childhood Couldn't Stop His Success)—youtube.com

What Happened to The Player Who LIED His Way Into the NFL?—youtube.com

Whatever Happened to…. Larry Brown—Sportscolumn.com

www.ingramcontent.com/pod-product-compliance
Lightning Source LLC
Chambersburg PA
CBHW060525130626
46553CB00002B/650